ововоч

# The Youngest Brother

# The Youngest Brother

◆

## On a Kansas Wheat Farm during the Roaring Twenties and the Great Depression.

*C. Hugh Snyder*

iUniverse, Inc.
New York  Lincoln  Shanghai

**The Youngest Brother**
**On a Kansas Wheat Farm during the Roaring Twenties and the Great Depression.**

Copyright © 2005 by C. Hugh Snyder

All rights reserved. No part of this book may be used or reproduced by any means, graphic, electronic, or mechanical, including photocopying, recording, taping or by any information storage retrieval system without the written permission of the publisher except in the case of brief quotations embodied in critical articles and reviews.

iUniverse books may be ordered through booksellers or by contacting:

iUniverse
2021 Pine Lake Road, Suite 100
Lincoln, NE 68512
www.iuniverse.com
1-800-Authors (1-800-288-4677)

ISBN-13: 978-0-595-35130-5 (pbk)
ISBN-13: 978-0-595-79832-2 (ebk)
ISBN-10: 0-595-35130-1 (pbk)
ISBN-10: 0-595-79832-2 (ebk)

Printed in the United States of America

*It takes a family to raise a child.*
This book is dedicated to my families—
the one I grew up in, and the one my loving wife and I reared.

# Contents

Preface . . . . . . . . . . . . . . . . . . . . . . . . . . . . . . . . . . . . . . . . . . . . . . xiii
1. Lightning . . . . . . . . . . . . . . . . . . . . . . . . . . . . . . . . . . . . . . . . . . 1
2. Insomnia at an Early Age . . . . . . . . . . . . . . . . . . . . . . . . . . . . 3
3. Old Shep . . . . . . . . . . . . . . . . . . . . . . . . . . . . . . . . . . . . . . . . . 5
4. My Heroine . . . . . . . . . . . . . . . . . . . . . . . . . . . . . . . . . . . . . . 6
5. Winter Apples . . . . . . . . . . . . . . . . . . . . . . . . . . . . . . . . . . . . 8
6. Homemade Bread . . . . . . . . . . . . . . . . . . . . . . . . . . . . . . . . . 9
7. Someone's in the Kitchen . . . . . . . . . . . . . . . . . . . . . . . . . . 11
8. When Mother's Gone . . . . . . . . . . . . . . . . . . . . . . . . . . . . . 13
9. Buying Groceries and Things . . . . . . . . . . . . . . . . . . . . . . . 14
10. Harvest . . . . . . . . . . . . . . . . . . . . . . . . . . . . . . . . . . . . . . . . 16
11. Chickens . . . . . . . . . . . . . . . . . . . . . . . . . . . . . . . . . . . . . . . 20
12. Keeping Warm . . . . . . . . . . . . . . . . . . . . . . . . . . . . . . . . . . 22
13. Peddlers . . . . . . . . . . . . . . . . . . . . . . . . . . . . . . . . . . . . . . . 24
14. No Ears . . . . . . . . . . . . . . . . . . . . . . . . . . . . . . . . . . . . . . . . 26
15. A Pantry Shelf Staple . . . . . . . . . . . . . . . . . . . . . . . . . . . . . 28
16. Uncle Sam, Auntie, and the Maxwell . . . . . . . . . . . . . . . . 30
17. Mother Nature Provides . . . . . . . . . . . . . . . . . . . . . . . . . . 32
18. The Talking Machine . . . . . . . . . . . . . . . . . . . . . . . . . . . . . 34

| | |
|---|---|
| 19. Face Down | 36 |
| 20. Night Ride Cancelled | 37 |
| 21. The War Game | 39 |
| 22. Union Valley | 41 |
| 23. "Fox and Geese" | 45 |
| 24. Blackman—Whiteman | 46 |
| 25. Blue Northers | 47 |
| 26. Keys | 49 |
| 27. The Last Buggy Ride | 51 |
| 28. The Party Line | 52 |
| 29. R. F. D. No. 1 | 55 |
| 30. Beans or Else | 58 |
| 31. New Beds | 60 |
| 32. Fast-Forward Farming | 62 |
| 33. Butchering Time | 64 |
| 34. Static | 67 |
| 35. Sonny Boy | 69 |
| 36. The Runaway | 71 |
| 37. Organs | 73 |
| 38. Bigots | 75 |
| 39. Back to the Farm | 78 |
| 40. Turkey Shoot | 79 |
| 41. No More Log | 81 |
| 42. Sittin' in the Rain | 82 |
| 43. Westward Bound | 84 |

| | |
|---|---|
| 44. Business as Usual | 85 |
| 45. Chips | 87 |
| 46. Four Wheels—No Brakes | 89 |
| 47. The Government Helped | 93 |
| 48. Stop, Look, Listen | 95 |
| 49. Skip to My Lou | 97 |
| 50. Tin Lizzy | 99 |
| 51. The Champ? | 103 |
| 52. Are We Really Farming? | 105 |
| 53. A Broken Heart | 106 |
| 54. Poisoned to Life | 108 |
| 55. An Affair with Whiskey | 110 |
| 56. Rabbits | 113 |
| 57. The Turkey Roost | 115 |
| 58. Stranded | 117 |
| 59. The Hobo | 118 |
| 60. Dug Wells | 122 |
| 61. Coming of Age | 124 |
| 62. Times Change | 126 |

# *Acknowledgments*

My thanks go to my daughters for their suggestions and editing, and to my darling wife who spent many lonely hours while I worked on these stories. I am indebted to Gerald Hedges for proofreading the manuscript. And I owe special thanks to Robert E. Lee, editor of a column in *Community,* a supplement to *The Daily Oklahoman.* It was he who planted the idea for the book.

# *Preface*

Memories, memories. The mind is a wonderful thing. It stores nearly unlimited bits of data, waiting for recall. I have selected these excerpts from my childhood and youth. Often over the years, however, details fade and leave our mental images either incomplete or somewhat distorted. The tales I relate are true as I recall, but I cannot vouch for their absolute accuracy—it has been a long time.

Life on the farm was sometimes trying but never dull. My father descended from a long line of Pennsylvania Dutch farmers who lived largely off the land. In the early days of America, their farms were virtually self-sufficient. Often we lacked the wherewithal to complete the job at hand and had to improvise. Those were the times we relied on Dad. In retrospect, I believe that being forced to improvise helps build character and self-esteem.

I have never regretted the trials of my youth and have always relished the triumphs. I hope these tales give you insight into life as we knew it on the farm many years ago.

*—Hugh*

# 1. Lightning

I peered through the bedroom door and saw Dad lying on the bed, flat on his back, but I didn't really comprehend what the clamor and trauma were all about. I was fourteen months old, and recollection of what happened that day is hazy. But as the years rolled by, the events were cemented in my mind as I heard the story repeated over and over.

On every farm in our part of Kansas, a windmill mounted on a tower pumped water for the family. The windmill was usually the tallest structure on the farm. About every farm house had a wall telephone on a party line. During a thunderstorm, the windmill and telephone were probably the two most dangerous things on a farm. A windmill was always an invitation to lightning strikes. The telephone jangled incessantly with each bolt of lightning, and the phone could give you a deadly shock if you were near it or talking on it during a storm. Our windmill was mounted on a wooden tower, with a heavy wire leading down, and fastened to a lever for throwing it "in and out of gear." On one August afternoon, it was turning full blast when our family returned from a shopping trip in town. A heavy thunderstorm was approaching, so Dad went to shut the windmill down.

Just as he grabbed the lever—"Flash! Boom!" A bolt of lightning struck the windmill. The charge traveled down the wire, entered his right arm, crossed his body in a path missing his heart, and passed to the ground through his left leg. The jolt threw him to the ground where he lay seriously injured but still conscious.

Mother, my older brothers, and our family's hired hand managed somehow to get Dad into the house and on the bed. In spite of the fact that using the telephone during a thunderstorm was usually a no-no, Mother telephoned our country doctor.

The hired hand, who was staying in the house, was so traumatized by the event that he cut the telephone wire on the porch where it crossed above the door and entered the house. He said he didn't "have to stay in the house with that contraption."

My Aunt Sarah, Dad's sister, lived three-quarters of a mile away, and we wanted to get in touch with her, but our phone was no longer in operation.

Mother sent my two older brothers, Lyle and Oscar, to trudge the distance through the muddy roads and carry the bad news to her.

The doctor determined that the charge had shattered the bone in Dad's lower left leg inside the rubber boot he was wearing. The bone was so badly splintered and the flesh so badly burned that the doctor could do little more than keep it clean and let it grow back as best it could.

During all the excitement, nobody paid attention to me because I was of no help and was kept out of the way. Nevertheless, I knew things were bad. Two things I do remember—though not as things in motion as they were happening—but as static pictures. I am peering through the bedroom door and can see Dad suffering in pain lying on the bed. Later, I am standing on the porch behind all the gigantic adults, gazing upward at the cut wire over the door.

Dad never tired of repeating the events of that day. When visitors came by after Dad was up and around, he would drag out the clothes he was wearing when the lightning hit. His trousers and shirt were shredded, as was his left rubber boot. The electrical current had melted brass nails in the heel of the boot. Slits in the boot were ragged as I remember them, but Dad said that at the time the slits were so clean and sharp that they could have been made with a knife.

One of Dad's favorite stories was about his hired help. After the hired hand had cut the telephone wire, he disappeared, and the next morning he was nowhere to be found. He had left without collecting his pay and we never heard from him again.

The shattered leg left Dad crippled, so he rented most of the farm to a neighbor until Lyle and Oscar were old enough to help in the fields. But he took it all in stride and lived an active life until after I was grown, walking with a cane the rest of his life.

# 2. Insomnia at an Early Age

During the hot Kansas summers, milk sours rapidly and butter quickly becomes rancid if you don't keep them cool. But we were extremely fortunate on our farm. When Dad drilled our well, he struck water at twenty-two feet and stopped drilling at only sixty feet—quite shallow for wells in the area. Water at that depth is much colder than at the depth of most of our neighbors' wells.

Dad, being the genius he was, took advantage of the cold water and built a milk house right next to the well beside the windmill tower. Inside, he built a wooden milk trough about two feet wide, two feet high, and eight feet long. He piped the cold water directly from the well into the trough. To keep the cool water flowing, he put in an overflow to carry water from the trough to the livestock watering tank out by the pasture fence. The trough did a great job of keeping milk and butter cool, and the cold water was ideal for cooling watermelons and cantaloupes.

Typical of most windmill towers, ours consisted of four corner posts and a network of horizontal and diagonal braces. All of us kids called the horizontal braces squares. Of course, the tower had to have a ladder up the side for servicing the windmill.

The tranquil twilight of a cool summer evening was great for doing those things kids must do, and the ladder along with all the bracing made a great place for us to play. One of our favorite pasttimes was to climb to the lowest square, walk around it while hanging to the diagonal braces, and lie back on the milk house roof—a stunt that didn't always please Mom and Dad. But kids will be kids, so Dad sawed off the lower four feet or so of the ladder to make the lowest rung out of reach for us little ones.

I was about five years old and, because of the missing rungs, could no longer make it alone. But my brother, Forrest, could. Being the good-hearted big brother that he was, on that summer evening Forrest boosted my sister, Mildred, and me to that first rung, and the three of us made it to the milk house roof to lie there in the cool twilight.

Along the northwestern horizon, distant lightning occasionally lit up the sky, but it was far, far away. Not far enough away, however, to quell Mother's fear when she came to the back door and saw us up there. She ordered us down in no uncertain terms. The memories of Dad's traumatic experience with lightning had instilled in all of us an extreme fear and respect for the phenomenon.

After Mother ordered us down, Forrest chirped, "We better hurry; lightning is going to strike the windmill. I can tell."

This little brother viewed Forrest as somewhat psychic and quite a genius himself—almost as good as Dad. I trusted him implicitly, never questioning his wisdom, and we began our descent. Forrest and Mildred scurried down and were lying on the cellar several feet away. But I, being the littlest one, was also the slowest; I had reached the bottom rung when, "Flash! Crash!" Lightning struck.

"I'm struck, I'm struck," I cried.

I recall the rest only from hearing Mother tell it as years rolled by. The lightning had been close. It struck a fence post less than a quarter mile away. Because I was frozen to the ladder, I had to be pried loose. The fear and trauma wouldn't go away. I continued to shiver and cry. Mother took me to bed with her where I quivered and whimpered through a restless night, unable to shake the belief that I had suffered the same fate as Dad.

# 3. Old Shep

Although the scar he gave me remained for many years, my faithful and loyal collie, Old Shep, remained my friend.

Our school was a half mile east and a mile north of our house. It was a typical early American one-room schoolhouse with a barn and two traditional mini structures at the back of the school yard. Most students walked to and from school, but the barn was there to stable horses for those who rode horseback or carts.

As a tot, I guess I was eager to start to school. When I was five years old, Mother let me walk part of the way to school one morning with my brothers and sister. When we were about a quarter of a mile from the school, Old Shep and I turned around and headed home. Part of Mother's bargain was that Old Shep would go along to see that I made it back safely.

Old Shep and I romped and played. Sometimes when we got tired, we would lie down together and rest. Once when we were resting, I decided that a pillow would be comfortable. The best substitute readily available was Old Shep. Although he normally was a gentle dog, the idea didn't set too well with him. He swung around and sunk his teeth into my cheek, drawing a lot of blood. The scar remained on my cheek for years, but we remained buddies, and I had gained a healthy regard for his feelings.

Dad had Old Shep trained to bring our cows in from the pasture at milking time, if they were in sight. When we could not see them, someone had to go after them. One of my earliest chores was to bring in the cows, and as you can guess, Old Shep always came along.

That was true until the evening he hadn't shown up. We called and called but no sign of Old Shep. We started scouring the barnyard, and we found him in some deep grass still alive but unable to get up from the pool of blood in which he was lying. Someone had shot him—where or why we don't know. He never recovered.

The scar from the Old Shep's bite stayed with me for many years, but the love for that dog healed the wound. I missed Old Shep, and shed some tears when he died.

# 4. My Heroine

Without her heroic efforts, only God knows what would have happened to us. Would we have remained a family or would each of us have had a different destiny?

When Dad was laid up from his bout with lightning, my older brothers and sister were still too young to be of much help around the farm, not to mention me as a toddler. Although Mom and Dad had rented most of the farm to a neighbor, someone still had to run the home place. Who?

Mother did. Not only was she nurse to Dad, chief housekeeper, cook, and mother to us, but Mom tended the chickens and livestock, milked the cows, and kept the home fires burning. She even learned to drive the Overland, although at the time, driving a car wasn't considered ladylike. But the terrific responsibility dictated that each of us help at the earliest age possible.

Dad recovered enough in a year or so that he began gradually to help with some of the chores, but his bad leg kept him from getting up and down easily, so milking cows was out of the question. Lyle and Oscar were milking cows by the time they were nine or ten years old, and Forrest and I followed shortly after, as our older brothers moved on to more responsible chores.

A hired hand did most of the work in the fields for a few years, but soon that, too, was taken over by my older brothers. Dad was eventually able to manage a team of horses and did some of the fieldwork, but any strenuous job that required using both hands while standing was more than he could handle. However, he was able to stand at a table or workbench and tinker to his heart's content.

Our milk had to be cared for—separated and cooled, and someone had to churn the cream into butter or prepare it for taking to market. We had a Bentwood churn that stood about waist high to an adult; I was churning butter when I could barely see over the top. But when the butter was produced, I got to drain off the buttermilk, and, boy, it was good.

And somebody had to do the washing. On wash day, Mother put a boiler over two burners of our stove. The stove was a three-burner Perfection kerosene model. Kerosene was in a glass container inverted in a well at one end of the stove. A valve in the top of the container—which was at the bottom when inverted—dripped the kerosene into the well to feed the burners. She brought the water to a boil. She then dipped the water out and carried it to the washer. Our washer had a wooden tub that moved up and down as you swung it from side to side and a fixed dasher on top of the clothes. As the tub moved both sidewise and up and down, it squeezed and agitated the clothes. Swinging the washer and turning the hand wringer were my jobs. After all the clothes were washed, we filled the tub with the first rinse and wrung them out again. The second rinse contained bluing. I often wondered how bluing made clothes white. Hanging them out to dry became my job sometimes after I grew enough to reach the clothesline.

All the work and stress took their toll on Mother. She was always tired and worn out. I remember one time when Mother was so exhausted that she collapsed on the floor in view of Mildred and me. We were really worried. The stress eased tremendously when my older brothers were able to take over the men's work, and Mildred was true help in the kitchen.

While Dad was laid up with his bad leg and renting most of the farm, cash flow was meager. Our horses grew old and some of them died. He had to mortgage the farm, even though at that time the economy was booming. But we all pulled through and remained a true family. We owe it all to Mother—one terrific woman—my heroine.

# 5. Winter Apples

Although Dad had planted a few fruit trees near our house, they included no apples. We had to drive some distance for apples since they did not do well in the semi-arid climate and black dirt in the "high country." Apple orchards were usually planted in spots near rivers or streams or where growers could irrigate them.

Every autumn, we bought several bushels of winter apples and stored them in the cellar. The apples were supposed to last until spring, but they seldom did. All of us kids loved apples, so when one of us got hungry, he or she went to the cellar and got an apple. The trouble was that we were always hungry—not because we didn't get enough to eat—we were just human.

One autumn day when I was five years old and my sister and brothers were in school, Dad and Mom loaded me in the old Overland touring car and we went to get apples. The day was cloudy and cold. Fall arrived early that year—almost like winter.

We drove the six-and-a-half miles into Pratt and at least that much farther to somewhere around Iuka. The long ride up was not the most comfortable in the open car without side curtains, but we didn't think much about it.

The apples we found were beautiful. We bought at least five bushels and had to have somewhere to haul them. We put two baskets in the rear seat, which left just a wee bit of seat for me. Then we closed the rear doors and dumped the rest of the apples loose on the floor. That filled most of the space in the rear, leaving things a little cramped. I not only sat on the little bit of seat left, but I also doubled up my knees under my chin and put my feet in that little bit of seat.

We were well into the afternoon when we began the long trek home, and the weather was getting colder. The windshield kept the wind off Mom and Dad and they seemed not to notice the cold. But where I sat, the wind blew in and around me. I was freezing, without room to move and stir up some circulation or to find a spot that was less cold. I just sat and shivered. I thought we would never get home. The warm house was certainly a relief when we reached home.

# 6. Homemade Bread

When baking day rolled around, Mother would get out the breadboard, flour, and other ingredients and start mixing bread dough. Bread, of course, needs yeast to make it rise. After she mixed the dough, she took out a little of it, put it in a glass jar, and stored it wherever the temperature was best—the cellar in summer and the pantry in winter. The stored yeast was the "starter" for the next batch of bread. If the yeast got too dry, cold, or hot, it would die.

Many rural families baked their own bread, and they also kept starters. Mother sent me over to our aunt's house to get a starter more than once. When someone's starter lost its punch, a neighbor or relative was always around to supply a new one. They simply divided their starter, which was ample for leavening two batches of bread.

After she mixed the dough and took out the starter, Mother left the dough to rise. When it had risen, she kneaded it back down, cut it into loaves, and placed them into baking pans to rise a second time.

While the loaves were rising, Mother prepared the stove and oven. The oven sat over two burners of the kerosene stove. First she checked the kerosene supply, and if need be, someone—often it was I—would go outside and fill the jug from the kerosene barrel. Next, she lifted the oven onto the stove. When the bread was ready to bake, Mother lighted the burners underneath the oven and baked it.

Mother wasn't the only person in the house who could bake. Dad was not a novice at baking either. Before Dad had moved to Kansas, he and his older brother, Adam, had operated a restaurant and bakery in Waverly, Nebraska, so when necessary, he baked the bread.

Coffee grinder Dad and Uncle Adam
used in their restaurant

We came to believe that whole wheat bread had better nutrition than white bread. Grocers didn't always carry whole wheat flour, so we tried making our own from wheat out of our granary. Dad had a coffee grinder he had used when he ran his restaurant, and it was still in good shape. It ground the wheat all right, but it was not fine enough to be called flour. What we really ended up with was cracked wheat bread, but it still was delicious and had more flavor than white bread.

Often our supper on Sunday evening consisted of fruit with bread and butter or some other light snack. But usually, it was something to relish.

A family of seven goes through bread like water goes through a sieve, so Mother did her baking routine two or three times a week. Occasionally, she baked on Sunday. On those Sunday evenings, supper was warm bread and fruit. If you have never eaten home canned peaches with home-baked bread, fresh from the oven and buttered while still warm, you have missed a real treat.

# 7. Someone's in the Kitchen

It was always a challenge. Sometimes Mother won; sometimes her offspring did. Often times, it seemed more like a game between Mother and us kids.

We sometimes gathered in the kitchen when work was slack or inclement weather kept outside work to a minimum. We all took turns helping Mother. I doubt that Mother called it help, but the rest of us thought we were helping.

On baking day, Mother frequently made biscuits (some people called them rolls). Another one of her specialities was cinnamon rolls. She rolled the bread dough flat, buttered it, sprinkled sugar and cinnamon on it, and maybe added raisins if she could find some. Then she rolled the dough up, let the cinnamon rolls rise, and baked them whole—slicing them after they were done. She said that if they were sliced and baked flat, the "goodie" would all run out.

Often Mildred and I would get into the act. Making cinnamon rolls was fun. We especially liked to help with them because we thought we could make them better. Mother had to watch the purse strings, so Mildred and I used the butter and sugar sparingly. We used as much as we dared without Mother intervening, because it made more syrup and improved the taste of the rolls.

As we spent time in the kitchen with Mother, Mildred and I honed our own baking skills. We had fun cooking for the rest of our family.

Mildred got hold of an especially good recipe for rolls, which became one of her specialties. I don't know what particular ingredients went into the rolls, but the recipe included nuts and, if she could find them, raisins. I do know that they were delicious. Cookies were often on the menu and candy, too. Popping corn in the evening was a favorite activity. My older three brothers led when pulling taffy or popping corn.

Mildred also baked cakes and was good at it. I'll let her tell it in her own words:

> When I was ten or twelve years old, I baked my first cake. It turned out very good, so from then on, I was the official cake baker in the family. When about fourteen years old, I said to Mother, "Mom, I want to learn to bake an angel food cake."

She said to me, "Don't ask me to teach you to make an angel food cake. The only one I ever baked was so bad the family used it for a football."

My father who, together with his older brother ran a bakery for several years, was sitting in the room, and he said to me, "I'll teach you to make an angel food cake."

So using only a table fork, I started beating the egg whites. Every minute or two I asked, "Is this enough?"

He would say, "No, beat it some more. Finally he said, That will do." Then he told me each step to follow to finish the cake.

The next week when my mother went to town, she bought an egg beater and said to me, "This is for you to use to bake your cakes." From then on, baking cakes was a little easier."

Doughnuts became my specialty. I usually made them when supper was done. Doughnuts worked best if baked in cold weather when we had a fire in the coal range. It got hotter than the kerosene stove. I dug lard out of the lard can, enough to fill an old iron kettle about half full. Then I removed a cover from over the firebox and placed the kettle over the hole, removing the cover to let more heat into the kettle. Then I mixed the dough—I knew the recipe by heart—and cut out the doughnuts. When the grease was hot, I dropped in the doughnuts, a few at a time, pacing them so that I could tend them without overcooking. I usually had a little help. Often someone else made some twists or odd shapes. We also would fry a few doughnut holes.

We all waded in on them. Occasionally, we had some doughnuts left for breakfast but often we didn't. Seven hungry mouths can consume a lot of doughnuts in a short time.

Forrest, Mildred, and I loved raw raisins, and we ate them every chance we had. Forrest was especially fond of them. Mother soon learned that if she wanted raisins for cooking, she had to hide them where we couldn't find them. Hiding them made finding them a challenge. It seemed more like a game. Sometimes Mother won, but sometimes her children did.

# 8. When Mother's Gone

Dad was as glad as the rest of us when Mother arrived home. But he did fine and made life interesting for the rest of the family.

Not often did Mother leave the rest of us at home while she took a jaunt elsewhere, but it did happen a few times. When we were little and she did go away, Dad took over. Since he and his brother, Adam, had run the restaurant and bakery, he really wasn't lost in the kitchen.

Having been raised in a Pennsylvania Dutch family, he liked some of their traditional dishes. They are strong on fried foods. I wasn't very fond of fried bread, but Dad's fried apples were out of this world. He liked his lettuce wilted and seasoned with bacon grease, but the rest of us ate our lettuce raw, sometimes with homemade dressing.

Our bread consumption didn't drop much with Mother gone, so baking duties also fell to Dad. That's when he really showed his talent gained in his bakery. The difference in what we kids remember about Dad's baking is amazing. Oscar says that Dad baked better bread than Mom. It all tasted good to me. Mildred remembers that Dad sprinkled water on the hot bread right out of the oven and wrapped it in cloth, which made the crust softer. But the part that impressed me was his technique. When the dough was ready for its second kneading to make it into loaves, Mother slashed off one hunk at a time and shaped it into a loaf. Dad slashed off two loaves at a time and kneaded one with each hand. Dad certainly looked professional in the kitchen, at least to me.

Other than the cooking and baking, things coasted pretty much as usual with all of us doing our assigned chores. But we did miss Mom and were glad when she got home—Dad as much as the rest of us. But Dad had done fine and made life interesting for us kids.

# 9. Buying Groceries and Things

Until the late 1920s, all businesses in Pratt were locally owned. We knew most of the owners personally. We went to a grocery store to buy groceries, to a drugstore to buy medicine, to a clothing or department store to buy clothes, to a hardware store to buy hardware, to a furniture store to buy furniture, and to a lumberyard to buy lumber.

The drug store had a soda fountain where you could buy soft drinks and ice cream. I remember my first cone. I tried to eat the ice cream out of the cone until Mom told me to eat the cone and all.

Duckwall's five and ten cent store sold candy that it displayed in glass bins. We always tried to talk Mother out of a nickel or dime to buy candy, and we usually succeeded. We looked over all the bins and pointed to our candy selection. Then the clerk scooped some out, weighed it on the scales, and then put it into a paper sack. Candy was always a highlight of our trip to town.

Hardware stores sold screws by the dozen or gross and nails by the pound. The clerk, who often was also the proprietor, counted out the screws. He weighed the nails, tore off a square of wrapping paper, folded it into a sack like cone, and poured the nails into it. He then folded down the top and tied the package with a string.

A few items in a grocery store were prepackaged, such as Quaker Oatmeal, Post Toasties, and Nabisco Shredded Wheat, but most things were sold in bulk. If you asked for ten pounds of sugar, the clerk, again often the proprietor, popped open a paper sack, scooped about ten pounds of sugar into it, and put the sack on the scales. He then sifted in enough sugar to bring the weight up to ten pounds. He folded the top of the sack over and tied it with string. The same was true for most items. Cookies and most fruit sold by the dozen. Bananas, which weren't always available, were shipped by the bunch and sold by the pound. The grocer hung the bunch and used a hooked knife to cut off as many bananas as you wanted.

Most grocery stores took orders by telephone and delivered groceries to city residents. The delivery truck generally used was a Model T Ford with a double deck bed open on the sides. It was dubbed a "prune wagon."

## 9. Buying Groceries and Things

W. E. Jett Mercantile was the town's only department store and consisted of three levels. Jett's was to Pratt what Marshall Field is to Chicago. The basement was a sophisticated variety store that was similar to a five and dime store. The ground floor had clothing and dry goods, and the upper floor featured other types of merchandise. You could ride an elevator, which was the only one in town, between the store's floors. All of us kids always thought it was a treat to ride the elevator, but Mother was hesitant at times and always saw to it that we stood in the back. The elevator door was a folding iron grill. If you stuck your arm through the grill, it could sever your hand.

Chain stores began invading the city in the 1920s. First it was Woolworth. J.C. Penney was next, followed by Safeway grocery. The chains made it tough on local merchants.

Jett's also had a grocery store in a one-story extension on the back. It had a mezzanine above the counter. On this mezzanine Jett's had its order desk. Flossie Farmer sat at the desk taking orders by phone, and her melodious voice always enchanted me. I could hardly take my eyes off her and was nearly oblivious to whatever else was going on. Truly, I had my first crush on Flossie.

# 10. Harvest

Nothing in early America was more jubilant or more cherished than the harvest, and for country folks, this excitement continued well into the twentieth century. Musicians, poets, and painters recorded its beauty and fascination in song, verse, and landscape as precious gifts to posterity.

Most of the arts, however, were directed to the autumn harvest that inspired poems like Riley's "When the Frost Is on the Pumpkin," and "The Fodder's in the Shock," and Helen Hunt Jackson's "October's Bright Blue Weather." It's the time of year when weather is at its best, and the harvest moon remains bright and full longer than in other seasons. But for a Kansas farmer, wheat harvest came in mid-summer and was a hard, hot, and dirty job. The farmer's reward came just after the harvest was over. That's when wheat farmers are most affluent and make their most expensive purchases.

In the spring we overhauled our harvesting implements as the wheat grew, headed, and ripened. For cutting wheat, many farmers had headers, and most had binders. We had no header, so if we chose to head, we hired it done for so much per acre. The header was principally comprised of a platform, an elevator, and a boom on the rear for driving it. Four horses pulled it, two on either side of the boom and behind the platform where they wouldn't trample the uncut wheat. The operator straddled a wooden bar connected to a wheel at the rear end of the boom. He swayed from side to side to steer the header. A lugged bull wheel with an attached sprocket and chain drove the working parts of the machine with true horsepower. The working parts consisted of a cutting bar, a reel to knock the grain back on the platform, and canvasses to carry the grain along the platform and up the elevator where it was thrown into a horse-drawn header barge. When the barge was full, another was ready to take its place. The full barge was unloaded onto stacks to be threshed later. The stacks resembled huge loaves of bread.

The field crew consisted of the header operator, stackers and at least two barge drivers.

## 10. Harvest

They all had to eat, so we have to include the woman of the house, Mother, as part of the crew. I was too young to make the field crew, so Mildred and I did what we could to help Mother.

Binding took fewer people than heading and took considerably less teamwork. The crew consisted of an operator on the binder and two or three shockers. Many farmers had enough family members to go it alone. A two- or possibly three-horse team pulled the binder, which was also driven by a bull wheel that operated a cutting bar, reel, and canvasses. However, instead of an elevator, the binder had a knotter for tying the grain into bundles and a kicker that knocked the bundles onto a bundle rack. The operator dropped the bundles in windrows to be placed in shocks that shed the rain. I first tried my hand at shocking when I was barely able to lift a bundle.

Heading had an advantage over binding in that it left fields clear so we could begin fall plowing early to conserve moisture for next year's crop. Good arguments for binding were that it took less hired help and that the grain could be cut a little greener, since, in shocks, the heads of wheat were exposed and the grain ripened without rotting or mildewing. Early cutting also gave some insurance against losing the crop to hail. Either way, the grain was now waiting for the thresher.

When we heard a rumble disturbing the quiet of the countryside, we ran out to see what it was. A steam engine was belching smoke and churning along the township road at two or three miles per hour dragging behind it a giant thresher, often referred to as a separator.

Where the road crossed a draw near our house, the township had installed a wooden culvert made of four planks nailed in a square. The heavy steamer with its boiler full of water was too much for the culvert. Anyway, the steamer crew got the machine across and left the repair of the culvert to the township.

The engineer always had to be alert for low telephone lines crossing the road or an entrance into a field. If a line were too low, someone would get up on the thresher and hold the line up with a pitchfork while the thresher went under it.

Since prevailing wind in Kansas from the south, the thresher was always set facing south with the blower that stacked the straw pointing in a northerly direction. That way it blew straw, chaff, and dust away from the work area. The crew unhitched the engine, the engineer turned it around, and they belted it to the thresher. Something about the engine that always intrigued me was the two whirling steel balls above the boiler. The steel balls were weights for a governor that controlled speed of the engine.

When threshing header stacks, the feeder that fed the cut wheat into the thresher was placed between stacks. When threshing bundles, the machine was placed wherever the farmer wanted his straw stack.

The thresher crew included the engineer, a separator man to run the thresher, and a water monkey to haul water to the steam engine. For threshing from stacks, supporting crew included several grain haulers and pitchers to feed the stacks into the hungry machine. Threshing bundles required bundle haulers, pitchers to help unload the racks into the machine, and spike pitchers in the field to help load the racks.

Feeding a crew of this size was more than most farm kitchens were prepared to handle, so the crew also included a cook. Most of the crew ate in the cook shack. The shack was a little wooden house on wheels and undoubtedly contained a stove and dining table. As a little kid I always stared at the cook shack in awe, wondering just what it looked like inside and what was in there. When my brothers were old enough, they became part of the crew, but they ate at home.

When a grain wagon was filled, another was waiting. The full wagon went to the granary and the driver scooped the wheat into the bin. The door to the bin was built so that as the bin became fuller, you added boards to the door to raise the level. This meant scooping the wheat higher as the bin got fuller, which was harder work.

One year we had a hotheaded grain hauler who was extremely foulmouthed. Forrest nicknamed him "Swear-Cuss," and the name stuck. My oldest brother, Lyle, who was also hauling wheat, had just finished unloading when the bin became so full that he added a board to keep the grain from spilling. As Lyle pulled away and "Swear-Cuss" pulled up to the door, the new board came crashing down.

I had been watching the show, so when the board came down, I thought it was odd because the board should have stayed there. I asked, "Did that board fall or did you take it out?"

"I took the…thing out…" and I won't repeat all the rest of what he said.

Once the threshing started, the water monkey was busy going from barnyard to barnyard pumping water from livestock watering tanks. As I watched the water level in our tank drop, I worried about where our poor cows and horses would get water. The water monkey assured me that Kansas wind always solved that problem, and he was right.

When the grain was all threshed and in the granary, it was ready to take to market. The night before we were to haul a load to the elevator, we pulled the wagon into the granary and loaded about sixty bushels of grain. Bright and early the next morning, we hitched a team to the loaded wagon and headed six-and-a-half miles away to town. I often went along.

The horses walked to town and the loaded wagon rode smoothly. When traveling home, the team often trotted with the empty wagon, and the ride was anything but smooth. We would get home about noon, eat, scoop on another load and head for town. Two loads made a very full day and a couple of tired souls.

But it was payday and that made it all worthwhile.

# 11. Chickens

Our first chicken house that I remember was a decrepit, old two-room gabled structure with a door to each room facing west. Every day when the weather was decent, we let the chickens out to roam the barnyard. They really loved to get outside, so when you opened the door, you moved quickly out of their way or they were all over you. At sunset, they returned to their house on their own to roost, and we shut them in for the night. In cold or wet weather, they remained cooped up inside.

Chickens provided us with eggs year-round and supplied us with meat—especially in summer. Gathering eggs was a daily chore on the farm. Mother gathered eggs most of the time when all of us kids were little, because they were less likely to get broken that way.

Eggs and chickens were also sources of income. We took live chickens to market in crates or gunnysacks. Because egg production was not great, we never needed crates for the few we sold—we took them to town in a bucket. Mother kept our eggs fresh, storing them in the cellar in hot weather. The grocer was always delighted to get our fresh eggs and traded groceries for them. He allowed Mother two cents a dozen more for the eggs than he sold them for. Customers clamored for fresh eggs, which they preferred to the inferior cold storage eggs.

Chickens may know enough to come in out of the rain. However, they don't always recognize the threat of an approaching Great Plains thunderstorm. Whenever a storm loomed nearby, the family joined forces and herded the chickens toward shelter. But once the rain started, the chickens cooperated and headed for shelter. Quite often we never got them to safety until wind-driven rain beat down on us, soaking us to the bones. We tramped in the mud until the chickens were corralled. Then we returned to the house and donned dry clothes.

Feeding the chickens was another daily chore. In the early years, we fed them mostly grain. We scattered it on the ground near the hen house when the chickens were outside and in the straw that covered the floor when they were confined during inclement weather. Feeding the chickens often was my job. As raising chickens became more sophisticated, we began feeding them a balanced diet. Production improved.

An unusually violent thunderstorm blew in one day. After the chickens were inside, we took refuge on our screened porch and watched the storm rage. It reached the point that we could see only a silhouette of the hen house because of the heavy downpour and blowing rain. Suddenly, the building rose several feet in the air before it collapsed and settled to the ground. Most of the chickens survived, but they roosted outside for a few nights.

The event created the need for a new chicken house. We built one facing south with glass cloth in front. It had roosts, dropping boards, and built in draft-free ventilation. It was really state of the art.

One spring, Mother noticed an unexplained decline in egg production. The kids knew why. Easter was approaching and we were snitching eggs out of the nests and hiding them around the yard. Each of us had to remember where he or she hid them.

On Easter Sunday, we all went out and gathered the eggs, which filled a twelve-quart milk bucket. None of the eggs had spoiled, but some were aged enough to flatten out when broken. They were so stale that Mother wouldn't think of taking them to market. What do you do with so many eggs? You eat them. We had scrambled eggs for breakfast and dinner. For supper, we ate scrambled eggs. We grew tired of eggs. Never again would we hide them.

Roosters often fight each other; I guess each wants to rule the roost. I was never too concerned when two of them picked on each other. What did disturb me as a kid was when a rooster picked on a hen; the male just wasn't supposed to pick on the female. So one day I was close to a pair out in the barnyard when the rooster jumped on the hen and started pecking her comb. I grabbed him by the tail and pulled him off her. The hen turned around and started pecking back, obviously unhappy.

When I returned to the house and told Mother about stopping the fight, I didn't understand the odd look on her face.

# 12. Keeping Warm

I often wondered, "How could the family have slept through a shotgun blast so close to their bedside?" Maybe they were sound sleepers.

Every October or early November when weather became too cool for comfort, we dragged the old coal stove out of storage and set it up in the dining room. It added nothing to the decor of the room and took up living space, so when weather warmed up in the spring, it came down and went back into storage.

Each cold morning someone rolled out of bed and built a fire. Some stoves or furnaces with larger space for the fire could be banked to hold fire overnight. But we had to kindle our stove daily. When all of us kids were small and Dad suffered with rheumatism caused by the lightning strike, building the fire was Mother's job. First, she would shake the ashes from the grate to the ash pit. Then she would dip kindling in kerosene, lay it on the grate, put coal on top, and stick a lighted match to it. Soon the fire was roaring, sometimes getting the stove red hot.

The stove had a damper in the stovepipe to control the flow of hot air up the chimney. It also had an opening or draft in the door to the ash pit to supply air for the fire and a check draft at the base of the stovepipe to rob the fire of air. By judicious use of these drafts, we usually controlled the fire well enough to keep the room comfortable. We also had a coal range in the kitchen, which we used intermittently in the coldest weather to cook and to heat the kitchen. On cold days we confined our living quarters to the dining room and kitchen. Milder days let us spread into the living room.

But someone had to get the fuel into the house the night before. Big brothers had more responsible chores, so carrying coal and kindling became my job. I was toting in coal when I was too small to carry a full scuttle; I carried in a half bucket full and went back with a second container for enough to fill the scuttle. In the fall, we often had corncobs that made excellent kindling and were easy to gather and carry. When we had used up the clean cobs, I went into the hog pen and gathered up the ones left after the hogs had eaten off the grain. Eventually I had to go to wood. That meant splitting it with an axe or sometimes breaking weak sticks with my feet. Through it all I managed to keep all of my fingers and toes.

## 12. Keeping Warm

The house had no bathtub—not even a bathroom. We heated water in a kettle on the stove, poured it into a washtub, and added cold water to get a good temperature. During the summer, that was no problem. We simply used the washhouse or, during off hours, the kitchen. Winter confined us to the warmest room. We hung blankets over the backs of chairs to block off an area behind the stove that we used as our bathroom. It wasn't private, but it did hide the unmentionables.

When my older brothers became teenagers, they felt a need for more of a life of their own. We had a brooder stove for raising small chickens each spring. During the winter the stove was idle, so they hooked it up in an upstairs bedroom. We boys then had a private room all to ourselves.

Sometimes a chimney would soot up so badly that enough air couldn't get through to keep the fire burning and the stoves wouldn't draw. I don't remember any great problem that we had, but our neighbor did. The story as I heard it was that one of the older boys was trying to get a fire going one morning while the rest of the family were still in bed, but the stove wouldn't draw.

When they did get up, they found him cleaning soot off the floor and furniture, but the fire was roaring. Disgruntled because the chimney wouldn't draw, he had taken a shotgun, climbed onto the roof, and fired down the chimney. Reportedly that did the trick, but the procedure is not recommended.

I often wondered if indeed he did shoot down the chimney, and if so, did the shot awaken anyone?

# 13. Peddlers

Although he didn't have a yardstick, tape measure, or ruler, his measurements were amazingly accurate. And to Mildred and me, his method was entertaining to say the least.

Almost as regularly as we turned our calendar, salesmen from Raleigh's and Watkins called at our house to display their wares. Those two were regulars. They peddled home remedies, extracts, toiletries, and more. Seldom did one of them leave without selling us something. Two items we always kept on hand were Raleigh's camphor ointment and Watkins laxative tablets. We also bought lots of our extracts and other medications from them.

I don't remember either of them stopping by the farm with horse and wagon, but I know they once did. I vaguely remember Mother's remarking to one of them about using a car now.

Some of us kids always watched the men display their merchandise. We were amazed at how many items one had concealed in his display case, which resembled a large suitcase. The display carried one of each item the salesman had to offer, but he carried a supply of each in his car. Once he had taken our order, he went to his car and filled it.

Peddlers other than the two regulars showed up from time to time. A Fuller Brush man visited less frequently than others, and seldom did the same salesman show twice. I guess brushes lasted longer than extracts and medicines.

After harvest, we always got a few one-time visitors trying to sell gadgets that might work but probably weren't worth the money. These salesmen didn't hook us very often. Then there was a Menke's Grocery man who came by one day selling dried fruits and other foods that were slow to spoil. He showed us some of the biggest, juiciest, and prettiest prunes and raisins we had ever seen. We ordered some and they arrived later by mail. They were no better than the ones we bought from our local grocer. Live and learn.

But the salesman who I remember best came by one evening a little before sunset with a horse and wagon. He used an enclosed van to protect his wares from the weather. He wanted to know if we could furnish him meals and lodging for the night, so we let him put his horse in the barn, fed him supper and furnished a bed. He was selling yard goods. Next morning after breakfast, he brought in several bolts of cloth for display. Mother bought several pieces. Mildred and I were more concerned by the novelty of the experience than the business transactions, but my guess is that he was trading merchandise for board and room.

He didn't carry a yardstick, tape, or ruler. He measured a yard by holding one end at the tip of his nose and the other at arm's length, and the measurements were amazingly accurate. Mildred and I found his method amusing.

# 14. No Ears

The huge straw stack that rises in the wake of a thresher gradually settles with age but can stand for years if not burned or hauled away. The front of the stack rises rather abruptly while the rear trails off at a much gentler slope. For the most part, the stack sheds water quite well. But around the edges and under the thin tail, soil becomes moist, and the straw, serving as mulch, holds the moisture even through the hot Kansas summer. Water that does trickle through carries nutrients to the soil below. Since prevailing winds are southerly in Kansas, the straw stack tail always extends to the north and thereby is shielded somewhat from the full blast of the hot southerly wind.

The climate in Central and Western Kansas is far from ideal for gardening, but straw stacks can help. Digging down through the straw only a foot or two deep, you can find nice, rich, moist dirt that stays moist all summer long, and just about anything that can take some heat will grow there. For several summers, Oscar dug holes in the straw and planted squash, watermelons, pumpkins, and other vegetables normally grown in "hills." Most of them produced quite well. They were some distance from the house, so it took frequent jaunts on foot or by auto to take care of them. Bugs were the biggest problem.

One year we had a bumper crop of pumpkins. We watched one pumpkin all summer as it grew and grew and grew, greatly surpassing in size any other in the stack. Time came to harvest the crop, and Oscar drove to the field taking Mildred and me along. We had waited too long. Someone had already harvested the big one and hauled it away. Our hearts were broken.

But we gathered the rest and loaded them in the back of the Overland. I was reminded of the time I rode home from Iuka with a load of apples. Mildred rode in a corner of the backseat with her feet in the seat and her knees to her chin in order to make room for the pumpkins. I rode up front with Oscar.

What do you do with a surplus of pumpkins? A family of seven can bake and eat only so many pumpkin pies, and we ate that many. We used many of the pumpkins in a way I have never experienced before or since. We cooked them to a pulp, spiced them up, and made them into pumpkin butter. The color and consistency was much like apple butter. The taste was not, but we ate it anyway.

## 14. No Ears

On the last day of October, I asked Mother if I could make a jack-o-lantern. She told me I was too young, and she was afraid I would cut myself with the knife. She also gave several other reasons why I should not. I persisted, and finally she gave in. However, I had to use one of the smallest pumpkins. It turned out fairly well—at least I thought so—and I was quite proud.

In the washhouse we stored grain in a tank, keeping it handy for feeding the chickens. After sundown, all of us kids proceeded to the washhouse where big brothers dug into the grain and pulled out one by one a jack-o-lantern for each of us. We lighted the candles, ran around hiding and then jumping out yelling, "Boo," and pretending to scare each other. We had quite a family party.

Another year I wanted to make a jack-o-lantern and was older and more experienced. I had no opposition from Mother. I thought it funny that a jack-o-lantern has only eyes, a nose, and a mouth. Why doesn't it have ears? Striving to be original, I cut an ear on each side, inserted a candle in the thing, and put a match to it.

Why doesn't a jack-o-lantern have ears? I had learned the hard way. To a jack-o-lantern with ears, the wind is like a mother's advice to her teenage daughter. It goes in one ear and out the other, and it snuffs the candle in passing.

# 15. A Pantry Shelf Staple

Sometimes you make do with what you have, but then when it's what most others in your realm have, you don't think much about it until the going gets really rough.

Ordinarily, we didn't think much about our routine treks to the little structure out behind the house. Every farmhouse had one. It took care of life's little necessities. Even here and there a house in town had one.

We had an especially nice two-hole unit. Ceiling boards lined the inside and lap siding covered the outside. It lacked the traditional half-moon air holes. Instead, the air holes were offset in the siding and interior lining so no one could peek in. The top of the seat was a single, wide, thick board. Holes in the seat were sawed at a bevel, and the pieces that were removed made excellent close-fitting covers that helped keep out flies and keep down unpleasant odors.

Twice a year we received catalogues from "Monkey" Wards and Sears Roebuck—a spring and summer and a fall and winter edition from each store. When we received a new catalog, the old one went to the little house out back. They usually lasted out the season and served their purpose well until sometimes when we got down to the color pages, which were slick and harsh.

When it was raining, we often put off our trips as long as possible. That was seldom a problem, although it did mean wading in mud since we had no sidewalks. Snow was worse. We either had to wade through the cold stuff or shovel a path. But wading was not the only problem. Kansas winds find a way to get snow through the tiniest cracks, and frequently snow covered the little house's floor and seat. The snow often melted a little and refroze. No way could you brush it off. When you bare those portions of your anatomy that normally are concealed, you sit lightly and hope your mission reaches a suitable conclusion.

I remember once when I was a preschooler we had a heavy snow with massive drifts. It covered our garden fence. When the surface hardened, I climbed the drift and slid down on the seat of my pants. It was great fun. It wasn't so much fun for Dad. He didn't shovel just a path. A drift across the path was higher than his head, so he shoveled a tunnel to the little house out back.

When it was really cold, we kids often put off our trip out back too long. When we did get up the nerve to go, we weren't always able to perform. It is little wonder that a staple always on our pantry shelf was castor oil.

# 16. Uncle Sam, Auntie, and the Maxwell

Dad sauntered up to the car and said, "Nice day, isn't it."

"Sure is," came the reply.

"Great," I thought, "things are as they used to be."

Saturday afternoon was a favorite time for farmers to go to town to buy groceries and other things they needed. My Aunt Emiline, Dad's sister, and her husband, Uncle Sam, kept a rigorous schedule. They rose and retired at the same times every day, and routinely made their Saturday trip to town immediately after noonday dinner. They lived about a mile-and-a-half from us, and on Saturday you could set your watch at one o'clock when you saw them drive up in the old, faded black Maxwell.

Auntie rode in the backseat, chauffeured by Uncle Sam. They no longer had children at home, so Auntie always asked Mildred or me to make the Saturday trip to town with them. Our place was in the back seat with Auntie.

Usually Mildred made the trip, but if she couldn't or didn't, I got a break. For some reason, one Saturday we both made the trip. The littlest one in the family seldom gets to ride up front unless it's on someone's lap, so riding in the front with Uncle Sam was a treat—I really felt grown up.

Auntie bought her bread at the bakery in town, and sometimes we had a chance to watch the baker in his routine. But we felt sorry for Uncle Sam and Auntie. They had to eat the soft, fluffy, tasteless stuff when we had real bread baked at home.

I don't know what model the Maxwell was, but it must have been about the same vintage as our 1917 Overland. The Maxwell was an open touring car, as were the majority of cars of the day, but it had one distinct advantage. It had permanently installed pull-down side curtains with celluloid windows, greatly simplifying the art of keeping dry when it rained and warm when it was cold. Many open cars had side curtains, but they had to be snapped in place one at a time—a wet job when it was raining and a cold one when it was snowing.

## 16. Uncle Sam, Auntie, and the Maxwell

Dad, Mildred, and I were visiting Auntie and Uncle Sam one day. Mildred and I were in the house with Auntie when Dad came in and said, "We have to leave—I've been ordered off the place."

We could hardly believe it! Auntie cried, but we left.

In spite of the tiff between the men, Uncle Sam honored Auntie's wishes and picked one of us up to go to town as usual on Saturday. But he didn't drive in the driveway; we had to meet them on the road in front of the house. This had been going on for several weeks when one Saturday, Uncle Sam pulled the Maxwell into the driveway to pick up Mildred. Surprise, surprise!

Dad warily sauntered up to the car and said, "Nice day, isn't it?"

"Sure is," came the reply.

What the tiff was about I'll never know, but that's water under the bridge. It was great to know that things were like they used to be.

# 17. Mother Nature Provides

When made into jelly, sand plums were luscious, but when we picked them, Mother didn't have to worry that we would eat more than we put in our buckets. They were too sour. Mother Nature provides an abundance of food, if one goes to the trouble to find it.

Two things we ate in spring and early summer, we found plentiful along the roadside. The plants are both weeds, but when they come up in the spring, they are tender. When cooked into greens they are good, if you like them.

We called one of the weeds, lambs-quarter—I don't know its true scientific name. Mother sent Mildred and me out in early spring to gather them along the roadside, with instructions to pick only the young ones. By early summer they grew pithy stems, and when we got home, we stripped off the leaves and threw the stems away.

The other weed was wild lettuce. Like leaf lettuce, it went to seed in a few weeks and was no longer fit to eat. It was not good raw, but when cooked, it was edible. I was never overly fond of lambs-quarter greens, but I preferred them to wild lettuce.

We never had wild blackberries in our area, but I heard people tell about picking them. I envied those who had blackberries to pick. However, we did have some wild fruit to gather.

Our part of Kansas had numerous ravines that were too sandy to till. When a farmer had a sand draw through his property, he usually enclosed it in his pasture. Wild sand plums grew in the sand. Farmers supplemented their incomes by selling the plums. We had no sand on our farm, so every year several of us went somewhere and picked a bushel or two, canned some plums and made jelly from the rest.

Some areas not too far from us were timbered, and among the timber you could find wild grapes. On occasion, we picked wild grapes. Picking grapes was more hazardous than picking plums, because you had to be alert for poison ivy and snakes. When made into jelly, wild plums and wild grapes are both delicious. Neither is fit to eat raw—they are too sour. That's why Mother didn't have to worry that we would eat more than we put in our buckets.

## 17. Mother Nature Provides

One thing that grew and thrived during the drought was the Russian thistle (tumble weeds). One fall they blew up against our garden fence and thoroughly seeded a sizable area of our garden. In the spring, we had a solid green mat of the things. We had heard of eating them as greens, so we tried it. We cooked some once, tasted them, threw them out, and finished the meal without greens.

# 18. The Talking Machine

The early "grapherphone" was driven by a spring motor that you wound up. Our first grapherphone was in three parts plus records. The main part was an oak cabinet structure that housed the spring motor and main working parts. It was seven or eight inches high and about fourteen inches square. The turntable was on the box and was removable. In addition, it had a crank and a horn assembly. You wound up the spring with the crank. A bracket on the side of the cabinet supported the horn assembly, which consisted of the horn and a diaphragm connected to a steel needle that rested on the record. Since the machine was not self-contained, storage of the various parts and records could be a problem.

To play it, you mounted the horn assembly, checked the needle, and, if necessary, replaced it. Then you inserted the crank, wound up the motor, and removed the crank. If you forgot to remove the crank, it turned backward as it played. You placed your desired record on the turntable and gently set the needle at the outer edge of the record and turned it on.

The spring had little more than enough energy to play one record. When you forgot to rewind it up, it soon ran out of "steam" on the next record. You couldn't rewind it while it was running, so you had to start over.

A speed control allowed you to vary the speed. No matter what the intended pitch, you could speed it up to a high-pitched screech or slow it down to a dragging bass. As I'm sure you can understand, playing with the speed control usually irritated others in the room.

Over the years the steel needle gliding over the record wore the record, and quality of sound deteriorated. Nonetheless, we listened to the records for many years.

One year our cousin and family, who lived close by, decided to leave the farm and move to St. Louis. They were in debt and had to dispose of some of their belongings to pay their bills. We helped them out by buying their round, oak dining table and their Brunswick console phonograph, which was much newer than our old one. By the 1920s, the name phonograph had pretty well replaced grapherphone.

## 18. The Talking Machine

What a difference a few years make. The replacement sounded much better, was easier to use, and was better looking. You could wind it while it played. Records were stored out of sight in the cabinet. The horn was permanently mounted in the cabinet out of sight. It had a volume control as well as a speed control. It also had a shutoff you could set to stop the machine automatically at the end of the record. Since all records did not end at the same radius, you had to set it before you started each record.

Electric phonographs made their debut in the twenties. Other than their power source, they differed little from their spring-wound ancestors. Our school superintendent bought a new electric console and donated his not too old one to the school.

Once during noon recess when the grand piano and the phonograph were both on the auditorium stage, I was playing the phonograph. Also on stage was one of our talented teachers, who was a whiz on the piano. When I started playing a number she knew, she wanted to play along, but the two instruments were not in tune. Sitting at the piano, she coached me as I changed speed to raise or lower the pitch. We finally got it in tune. The piano accompaniment sounded great, even to my untrained ear.

# 19. Face Down

"You can't come in the house like that. Get out of those clothes and clean up." That was Mother's command when I showed up at the door somewhat distraught and humiliated.

As most farmers can tell you, the ground around the livestock watering tank and near the barn is where most farmers feed winter roughage to their livestock. You can understand why the animals spend many winter hours in the area. Now cows and some other farm animals are not choosy as to where they perform life's little necessities and seem to relish in tramping in the area. Spring thaws and showers consistently turn the area around the watering tank into a marshy mess of some unpleasant chemicals.

One spring day was warm and beautiful, the kind that makes you want to get out and enjoy the fresh spring aroma of God's great outdoors. Oscar and I were doing just that when we strolled some distance from the barn into the pasture and up to our old white mare, Mag. She was a draft horse and as far as I know had never been ridden, but by this time she was out to permanent pasture. Being the gentle horse that she was, she allowed us to take liberties that a younger, more spirited horse would not. So without saddle, bridle, halter, or rope, Oscar boosted me onto her back and climbed on the horse behind me.

Carrying passengers was strange to her, and our presence on her back excited her into a flourish of exuberance. She took off at a full gallop and never slowed down until she reached the area around the water tank where spring rain and thaw had been at work. We had no trouble staying mounted during the first part of the trip, despite the fact that we had no control over Mag.

Suddenly near the water tank, she planted her front hooves, made a ninety-degree turn and stopped all in one quick maneuver. She and Oscar made the turn. I didn't. I landed face down in the marshy muck.

Mother's orders to go to the washhouse, bathe, and change clothes came as a welcome command. That was one bath I was glad to take, even if it wasn't Saturday.

# 20. Night Ride Cancelled

The wound was not hurting, but the evening had turned traumatic for me. I was in no mood for further gaiety.

No matter if it was a circus, a carnival, or an air show, it was conducted in some farmer's cow pasture. A pasture was the only available area with a firm ground surface of sufficient size for the event. And in our wheat farming community, it was scheduled soon after harvest when cash was most plentiful.

The circus traveled by train and arrived in town the day before the first performance. They recruited local people, usually high school boys, to set up the big top—a large tent with bleachers set up inside. The pay for helping set up the big top was a free ticket to the circus.

The first show was a parade down Main Street featuring the steam calliope, elephants, camels, clowns, horses, and cages housing the more violent lions and tigers. The parade was a great event in itself. We nearly always got to town to see the parade. Occasionally, we were treated with a ticket to the big top. One year, Forrest earned his ticket by helping set up the big top, but by the time I was old enough to try it, the Great Depression had confined the circus to markets more lucrative than those of small Kansas towns.

A carnival traveled in much the same fashion as the circus but without any animals. The Ferris wheel and the merry-go-round were always featured. Other rides varied from year to year. Sideshows, game booths, and shooting galleries made up the rest of the layout. Mildred and I always rode the merry-go-round, but Mother thought the Ferris wheel was too much for us in our younger years.

I remember witnessing one eye-opening event at the carnival. A man had scales and a box of cheap little bamboo canes. For a dime, he guessed your weight and you stepped on the scales. If he had missed your weight by more than a certain amount—I believe it was ten pounds—you got a "free" cane. A quite heavy woman walked up and gave him her dime. As she stepped on the scales, he guessed a ridiculously low weight and, without looking at the scales, reached for a cane and handed it to her.

Airplanes of the early and mid-1920s were biplanes with wings braced by struts and wire. We seldom saw one of the things, but if one did fly over, we all ran out to see it. They were not fast and usually flew low enough that we got a good look.

But they were maneuverable. Barnstorming pilots flew them upside down, looped them, spun them and put them through mock dogfights. Daredevils walked the wings and hung from the landing gear by their teeth. An air show was a real novelty and quite exciting.

Since pastures were wide open and the view unobstructed for a considerable distance, you could easily park some distance from the pasture and enjoy the show without paying. We were guilty of the sin at one show, parking in a field across the road with dozens of other freeloaders. Air show officials didn't think this was quite right and came across the road to politely ask us if we would pay up. Who could refuse? Dad paid up and we drove across the road and got a closer view of the planes.

When Lyle was in high school in Pratt, he drove an old Model T Ford touring car. It was the vintage that had a vertical windshield hinged in the middle, and you could fold down the top half. That summer a carnival came to town, and the family, along with our hired hand, had driven the Model T to town to celebrate. Mother finally conceded that Mildred and I were now old enough to ride the Ferris wheel. I was excited at the prospect, but not as excited as Lyle was when an airplane landed in the pasture beside the carnival. Nothing would do for Lyle but to drive across the pasture to get a close up look at that airplane.

We all piled in the old Model T and took out across the pasture; four in back and four in front where I sat on our hired hand's lap. The windshield was folded down. We hadn't gone far when a front wheel dropped into a hole and brought the car to an abrupt halt. I flew forward off the hired hand's lap and hit the edge of the windshield, breaking the glass and putting a bloody gash in my face. Our activities came to a standstill for a while. Lyle failed to get a close-up look at the flying machine.

My wound didn't hurt, but still the evening had turned traumatic for me. I was in no mood for further gaiety and declined to ride the Ferris wheel. I was grown when I finally took my first Ferris wheel ride.

# 21. The War Game

The battle was over when blood flowed. Other endeavors seemed safer.

A farm family was somewhat isolated from others, so they learned early to entertain themselves. When chores were all done and we had no other pressing duties, we found plenty to do. Manufactured toys and games were not always available, so we improvised.

The slingshot was a favorite. If one of us wanted one, he found a tree branch as near to a "Y" shape as possible. He cut notches at the ends of the top branches, and the bottom was the handle. Then he tied two strips of rubber from a discarded inner tube, using the notches to hold it tight. He fastened a leather pouch to the other ends for holding the missile. It worked great, but it took a lot of practice to learn to hit a target.

Another favorite was a sailing propeller. To make it, one took a No. 9 wire about three feet long, made a loop in the middle, and twisted the two ends together in a neat spiral. He cut a thread spool in half and slid half of it down the twisted wire. He made the propeller from a tin can lid. Using a nail about the same diameter as the wire, he punched a "figure 8" hole in the center that would slide down the wire as it spun around. He cut slits around the edge of the lid and formed the propeller blades. Here is how one flew the propeller. First, he dropped the half-spool down the wire and spun the propeller to the bottom. Then, he put a finger through the wire loop and held the thing high in front of him pushing up on the spool with all his might. The propeller gained enough speed to carry it several feet in the air and then came wafting down.

We bound our Kaffir corn with a corn binder and topped it—that is cut off the heads to be threshed for the grain. The rest of the bundle made fodder for livestock. A corn binder cuts the stocks at about a forty-five degree angle. Many stocks are an inch or more in diameter at the bottom, tapering off to about a half inch where headed at the top. Having been cut while still green, the stocks are heavier at the bottom than at the top. You could throw them with the heavy end first, like a spear. The remnants of leaves served as fins to guide the missile.

One time we had company with several boys among them. The four of us with our company made enough men to form two teams and have a battle with

Kaffir spears. We made our own rules. When a player got hit, he went to the other side, the object being to get everyone off the opposing side.

When you got hit, the diagonal cuts made the strike uncomfortable. The game was going great until one of our visitors took a hit on the temple. It drew blood. That's when we turned to a milder form of recreation.

## 22. Union Valley

Union Valley was the name of our one-room country school, and it was much like the traditional "little red schoolhouse" portrayed in early American literature. A three-member school board administered the school. They hired the teacher, purchased equipment, and approved improvements to the building and grounds. The school district held a school meeting of local residents each year and elected one member to serve for three years. School kids always looked forward to school meetin' day, because it meant no school, just an afternoon on the playground while the older folks attended to community affairs.

The building was a small, rectangular frame structure with three windows along each side and two in the rear. A potbellied stove and chimney stood in the center, making a sport of hiding behind it where the teacher couldn't see us, and there we would cut up.

About the time I entered first grade, the school added an entrance hall where we hung our coats, took off our muddy overshoes, and stored our lunches. A few years later when I was between the fourth and fifth grades, the school board replaced the potbellied stove with a circulating heater. The following summer they moved the chimney to the end of the building and set the heater to one corner of the room, destroying our hiding place.

The schoolhouse also served as a meeting place for other community affairs. We always put on a Christmas program, which just about everyone in the district attended. The last day of school brought most of them to another program and a potluck dinner. Several black families were homesteaders in or near the district, and one of them named the Williamses had two boys, Harrison Dean and Thomas, still in school. Their mother was the best cook around. Everybody was eager to see what Mrs. Williams brought. Sometimes we also had an end of school picnic, often combining it with a neighboring school.

Mother was secretary on the school board much of the time I was in school. Often some kid tried to gain clout by announcing his or her parent was on the school board. But my siblings and I were on strict orders never to mention that Mother served on the board. One fall, the board erected basketball backboards and hoops behind the schoolhouse, and Mr. Williams hitched his team of horses to a road drag and smoothed the court.

Harrison Dean, Thomas, and I were very good friends. Soon after the court was finished and we were playing on it, for some strange reason, Thomas said to me, "Hugh, I've got more right here than you; my dad dragged it."

"Oh, yeah," I shot back; "My mom's on the school board."

That evened the score then and there. And we still were good friends as always.

I never told Mother about the brief exchange. I know she would never have approved. What would she have done? Heaven only knows, and I don't like to think about it.

My first two years in school are almost a blank. In the third and fourth grades, my uncle was our teacher. I spent more recesses at my desk than I did on the playground. My report card showed excellent marks until it got down to conduct. There I failed.

But then I began to grow up. When most pupils needed to read an assignment two or three times, I read it once and was ready to recite. I began using my spare time to my advantage—drawing, writing, and using reference books.

When I was in the sixth grade, I had a poem, "The Seasons," published in the *Pratt Daily Tribune*. Needless to say, that inflated my ego.

In the seventh grade, I made a stab at writing fiction in "The Discovery of Toy Town." Charles Lindbergh had recently flown non-stop across the Atlantic. What could be more appropriate than an air adventure? When I had my story partly written, I showed it to the teacher. Nothing would suit her but that I tell it at the Christmas Program. When the fatal night came, I stared into the Coleman lanterns that lighted the room—stage fright keeping me from facing my audience—and related my story.

## "The Discovery of Toy Town"

"In November I got in Dad's airplane and started flying north. I knew the North Star was right over the North Pole and that Santa lived there. If I flew toward the star until it was right over my head, I would be over the North Pole. I could look down and see Santa's place. After a while I flew under clouds and could no longer see the North Star. I kept on flying north as best I could, but I was really lost. Then I began seeing snow on the ground under me, and it got heavier and heavier.

The trees were getting smaller and more scattered. Soon it was nothing but snow. I was really lost and didn't know how to get home.

My engine sputtered and died. I was out of gas. I was able to land the plane on the snow, but it was really cold and I had no way to keep warm. I was sure I'd freeze to death.

Then I saw a black place in the snow quite a way from my plane. I waded over to it to see what it was. It was a big hole in the ground, and warm air was coming out of it, melting the snow enough to leave the ground around it muddy. I got up closer to the hole to look in. My feet slipped out from under me and I started sliding down the hole.

When I hit bottom, I was at the end of a long street of a town in a big cave. At the other end was a big red house trimmed in white. Along each side of the street were houses with buildings behind them. I started down the street. From the houses and buildings behind them I could hear hammers, saws, sewing machines and other tools. I could smell cookies and candy cooking. It was a busy place.

I reached the big red house and knocked on the door. A large fat lady dressed in red came to the door. 'I'm Mrs. Santa, and you're in Toy Town. Santa would like to see you.'

She took me to him. Santa said, 'You've been a bad boy—taking your father's airplane without asking. What do you think we ought to do?'

I didn't answer.

'I tell you what,' he said. 'It's nearly Christmas and I'm really busy. If you will tend and feed my reindeer, it would help me a lot. That could help you make up for being a bad boy. You can stay here until Christmas.'

I took care of his reindeer and stayed at his house, but I didn't see Santa very often. I was afraid I wouldn't get any Christmas presents and didn't know if I'd ever see my folks again. Then a day before Christmas, Santa came to me and said, 'I'm giving you your Christmas presents early.' They included a suit of winter underwear, warm corduroy trousers, a fur-lined coat, a wool muffler, long wool socks, and warm, high-topped shoes.

On Christmas Eve, he had me put on all the warm clothes. 'You'll need them on the sleigh ride' he said.

He had me help him load his sleigh and then get in the seat beside him. Down the street we went and right up the hole I had slid down, and we were on our way. Santa really works fast. We dropped off our toys along the way until we reached my home. There he dashed into the house and I was right behind him. Mom and Dad were there and were really glad to see me again. They never knew what had happened to me. It was the best Christmas I ever had."

Santa never told me how to find the place again. I guess he was afraid that if the location ever became known, tourists would flock in and he could never get his work done.

# 23. "Fox and Geese"

At Union Valley we sometimes played a game called "Fox and Geese," but not often. It called for a level snowfall, one that wasn't too deep. Kansas winds usually pile the snow in drifts, seldom leaving it level enough. It was a game that both girls and boys played. No set number was required. It was open to all who were around and wanted to get into the game.

We tramped a circle in the snow somewhere between ten and fifteen feet across with two paths through the center crossing at right angles.

One person was "it" or the "fox," and the others, "geese." I don't remember how we chose the fox.

The object of the game was for the fox to catch a goose who then became the fox, and the fox metamorphosed into a goose. Both fox and geese had to stay on the paths tramped in the snow. You think it's easy? Try it. A goose can entice the fox into a path and then place a solid place between them. If the geese get too scattered or get into each other's way, the fox has half a chance. The game came to an end when the teacher rang the school bell.

## 24. Blackman—Whiteman

I had always thought that seeing stars when you were hit on the head was reserved for the funny papers. That's not always true.

At Union Valley we had two games that we played occasionally—Blackman and Whiteman. The significance of the names evades me. One good thing about them is that both girls and boys would play. We played Blackman most frequently. In either game, we had two bases. One was the side of the schoolhouse and the other, the side of the school yard. We picked a leader for each side and they chose sides. One side went to each base.

In Blackman, one person would be "it" and took the center of the field. Opponents would dash from home base, trying to evade "it" and reach the opposite base. If tagged by "it," he or she went to the other side. I can't recall the details of how we exchanged the position of "it" or how one returned to the base if he or she didn't get caught in the initial crossing.

Whiteman was a lot more active. Any or all players could cross at the same time. As I remember, any member could capture a member of the opposing side. But if that were the case, who tagged whom? I can't answer.

During my last year at Union Valley we had a young teacher who, I believe, received her teacher's certificate right out of high school by taking teachers' examinations rather than by attending college. She mixed with her students as much as feasible and during one recess played Whiteman with us. Everyone was darting around in evasive tactics to avoid being tagged. In the evasive maneuvers, the teacher and I collided, bumping heads solidly, and I went to the ground. Then is when I learned that seeing stars is not confined to the funnies. The stars come in different sizes and colors.

An old adage states, "Bump heads in the day, sleep together that night." I can assure you that the adage didn't hold true that night.

# 25. Blue Northers

The morning was beautiful—a bit breezy but unusually mild for mid-winter. We headed for school clad in light jackets and stocking caps but no overshoes or gloves.

Daily newspapers carried weather forecasts, but on the rural route the paper did not arrive until we were well into activities of the day. During my first six years at the school, the school had no telephone, so rural school kids were out of touch with the rest of world during the school day.

Early one day, without warning, clouds appeared on the northwestern horizon and soon a strong northerly wind—at least forty miles per hour or more—developed. Shortly after that, snow filled the air and drifts began building in sheltered areas.

We had little choice other than to brave the storm in our light clothing and walk the mile-and-a-half home. The wind was to our back the first mile, and an Osage-orange hedge lined the west side of the second half of that mile. The hedge offered some relief from the wind, but drifts piled up in its shelter, which meant we had to wade through deep snow. No way could we keep snow from getting inside our shoes where it melted and made our feet bitter cold. We walked west the last half-mile and the wind hit us from the right front corner. The east-west road was sheltered by tall grass and weeds in the fencerow, causing the road to drift full as typical of most east-west country roads. The last half-mile definitely was the worst part of the trek home. When we made it home, we sat down beside the stove and warmed our aching feet.

With slight variations, the story would repeat itself several times during the seven years that I attended Union Valley. One year when we had a male teacher, he had a way home so he loaned me his jacket; I might never have reached home without it.

One December night when my uncle was our teacher, we were putting on our school Christmas program with the usual Coleman lanterns to light up the place. This time the blizzard struck during the program. It didn't reach an intensity that kept patrons from driving home, but my uncle and his family had quite a distance to go—mostly on east-west roads—and could have been stranded in the storm. They elected to follow us home and spend the night with us.

Even in the short time the storm had been raging, the east-west, half mile route home had become impassable. But the field on the north side of the road had an entry at the corner and another across from our house. The ground was usually frozen during excessively cold weather, so we took to the field for that last half-mile. In fact, farmers and even the mail carrier often drove through fields when roads were blocked. Landowners expected it.

During my last year at Union Valley, Lyle and Oscar were attending high school in Pratt and were driving an old four-cylinder Essex that was equipped with side curtains in winter.

During the summer before, the school board had approved a party line telephone for the school, so the next time the storm caught us unaware, we could communicate. We were informed that no way could anyone get a car through the snowdrifts. Everyone stayed at the schoolhouse until one of the parents from north of the school arrived with a team of horses and a wagon. We all, including our teacher, huddled down in the grain bed and covered the bed with a tarp. It was really cozy. We were all to be bedded down with neighbors, and all parents knew where their children were—supposedly.

If anyone could get a car through the snow, it was Lyle, and he did. We weren't a half-mile north of the school when we met my brothers plowing through the snow in the Essex. Mildred and I got out of the wagon and climbed in the car.

About a quarter of a mile south of the school, we bogged down in the mud where the snow provided enough insulation to keep the ground from freezing. When we learned that we could not get moving again, we began the long, frigid walk home. Our socks got wet and our feet and hands got so cold that they lost all feeling. They were no longer hurting.

We were certain that, when we made it home and our feet thawed out, we would discover frostbite. When feeling began to return, my feet felt as though a thousand needles had probed them, and they felt worse before they felt better. But as always, we were all lucky. The pain finally subsided with no lingering after effects and no frostbite. Hallelujah!

# 26. Keys

Two times in my life, Dad took me over his knee. However, usually the severe discipline was left to Mother.

Our front door had a night lock so, when locked, you could open it from the inside. To open it from the outside, you needed a key. We had no key. Gadgets such as this lock always intrigue curious youngsters, and the Snyder kids were no exceptions. On occasion, somebody got locked out to the chagrin of Mom and Dad. Sometimes one of us kids locked another out just to be ornery.

The back doors and inside doors also had key locks but no keys. As a child, I often wondered why doors, especially inside ones, even had locks. None of our outbuildings had locks.

In order to keep cool during hot Kansas summers, we left all windows and doors open day and night as long as it wasn't raining. We didn't even draw the shades at night, much to the dismay of some of our city friends who occasionally came to spend the night. But who would be roaming the countryside at night to see inside? With windows open, we were lulled by the quiet of the summer evening that was broken only by the occasional chirping of a cricket or locust, by the distant baying of a coyote, or by the rustling of leaves.

Even when going to town, we left the house unlocked in case someone needed to get in. I can't remember the house ever being locked, no matter how long we were gone.

Open cars had no locks, although most of them were equipped with switch keys. Most people just left the key in the switch—it was easier to find that way. But if we did lose a key, we didn't have a problem. We simply took a screwdriver, disconnected the wire from the switch, and attached it to some positively charged terminal. And away we'd go. We wouldn't think of doing that to any car but our own.

Farmers went to town on Saturday afternoon, and the men often congregated on Main Street, trading stories of family, crops, politics, and things in general. One day our neighbor drove his black Buick Roadmaster to town. He parked on Main Street and left the key in the car. After about two hours, because of a parking limit, he moved his car to a side street to avoid a ticket, so he thought.

Later he went to the side street to get his Buick and go home, but no car was there. Had someone actually stolen it? Pondering his next move, he returned to Main Street. There he saw his big black Buick parked at the curb, displaying an ominous parking ticket.

One black Roadmaster looked much like another, and someone else had also parked one on Main Street and left the key in it. Our friend had saved the other man a ticket by moving the wrong car.

One lazy afternoon Mildred and I were playing in our front yard and scratching in the dirt, when we came across an old skeleton key encrusted with rust. We recognized it as a key and wondered if it really worked. It did, but not too well. We got the front door locked but couldn't unlock it. Dad finally took the door off.

Dad was a compassionate and gentle man. He would intentionally hurt no one. But he had told us repeatedly not to lock the door, so it was then that I went over the knee for a few good licks—just for locking the door. I never forgot the day—not that I suffered any pain, but because of the humiliation.

# 27. The Last Buggy Ride

Dad bought our first car, an Overland touring car model 75, after harvest in August 1916, about a month before he was struck by lightning. The thing created some extreme family excitement, and although I was only a little over one year old, the family's excitement caught on. What I remember of that day is a static picture. There I am, standing behind those gigantic people staring up at the monster that, from a toddler's view, towered to great heights. It was big and black and awesome.

At the time, seeing a car in the country was quite an event, much less owning one. For many country folk, the automobile would never replace the horse and buggy. Well, maybe it would in town but never on these rutted, often muddy, country roads. By the early 1920s, the bias against automobiles had softened. In fact, most farmers owned cars by then.

After Lyle and Oscar had completed the eighth grade, the rest of us kids usually walked the one-and-a-half miles to and from school, no matter what the weather. But one year we had a wet spring, so one rainy morning after we had trudged through the mud for days on end, Dad took pity on us and offered to take us to school. But navigation of muddy country roads still was much more suited to horse-drawn vehicles than to automobiles, so he hitched our old mares, "Nance" and "Bell," to the old surrey and we headed for school.

We sloshed along for three-quarters of a mile or so, listening to the rain pelting the top of the old buggy. Then without warning, the buggy began loping in a very strange fashion. On inspection, we found the rim of a rear wheel had parted from the spokes about half way around the wheel. We could hardly hope for the good fortune of getting to school on that wheel, so to take weight off the wheel, Dad had us get out. He turned the buggy around and headed for home while we plowed our way on foot through the mire.

Dad made it home without a load on the wheel. He parked the buggy behind the chicken house to rot away, and there it stayed along with idle farm machinery and outdated equipment. For the Snyders, the automobile had now totally replaced the horse and buggy.

# 28. *The Party Line*

Early country telephones were weird-looking contraptions. Like all rural phones, ours hung on the wall, and we had to stand when using it. It had two dry cell batteries inside, each about two inches in diameter and seven inches tall, that furnished current for talking. It had bells up front and a mouthpiece extending out from the center. On the left side was a fork, which held the receiver and connected you to the line when you lifted the receiver and "cut you off" when you hung it up. On the side opposite the receiver was a crank that turned a magneto, furnishing current to ring the bells on all phones on the party line. Each party had an identifying code of long and short rings. Our code was three short rings and a long ring. One long ring contacted the operator, and a series of short rings was a "line call," where everybody was supposed to listen. The line call usually was an announcement of some kind initiated by either an individual or the operator. One time we initiated a line call when the neighbor's barn caught fire.

The country telephone

## 28. The Party Line

Each line had many phones—ours had about sixteen. A single wire connected all phones on the line and each phone was grounded to the earth to complete the circuit. Sometimes the signal became so weak that hearing was difficult, especially if the batteries were low. The line, strung on poles, attracted lightning that sent a surge into the phone during a thunderstorm. The bells rang with each bolt of lightning. The surge packed a good wallop as well. No one went near the phone during the storm, except maybe in an emergency, as we did when Dad was struck by lightning.

Since the party line served all phones, nobody had any privacy. A favorite pastime for busybodies or curious neighbors was eavesdropping on conversations of others. Too many phones "off the hook" drained on the current, lowering the volume until you could hardly hear. This happened one time when Mother was talking, and she made the remark, "Too many people must be listening in. I can't hear." She then heard, "Click, click, click, click," as one by one the people hung up. Then she could hear quite well.

When any infectious disease struck a household, that place was quarantined for six weeks. Nobody was supposed to leave the premises. One winter, Lyle took down with the measles. About one week later as he was recovering, the rest of us kids got the disease.

Before the quarantine ran out but after Lyle was back to normal, along came a blizzard that caught us without groceries and other necessities. Dad had to take the wagon to town—quarantine or no quarantine. Making the trip alone would be miserable, so Lyle went along. That afternoon my aunt called Mother. Now Mother knew that the conversation was not private and also that none of us were supposed to leave the place. So when Auntie inquired about Dad and Lyle, Mother asked, "What did you say?" Auntie repeated the question, and Mother answered, "I can't hear you." Mother wouldn't lie. She couldn't hear with the receiver at arm's length from her ear. She hung up. Knowing Auntie would call back, she wedged cardboard between the bells and the clapper. That didn't silence the thing but changed the ringing to thudding, but Mother wouldn't answer it.

When Dad was young, he and his family spoke Pennsylvania Dutch in their home. One day he was talking to Auntie when the conversation turned to something that we kids weren't supposed to hear. We did hear it, but we didn't understand anything since they spoke in the language of their youth.

Our phone number was 2612 and our Uncle Elmo's was 2407 on a different line, so to call one another we had to go through the operator. One day Uncle Elmo was at our house and needed to call home. He rang the operator and gave her the number two-six-one-two. She told him, "Ring three shorts and a long on your line." He looked a little bewildered but obediently did as told. He received no answer. Mildred and I were giggling, because we knew what was happening. He soon woke up to his mistake and asked for two-four-o-seven. Our aunt answered.

Sometimes during a thunderstorm, an eerie thing would happen. I don't remember it, but Mildred remembers seeing it on more than one occasion. In her own words:

> Many times when lightning was close, the phone gave off "balls of fire" that rolled across the room fifteen feet more or less, popped, broke into pieces, and disintegrated. Sometimes they rolled into the next room. The whole phenomenon lasted only about four to six seconds. These eerie things gave me an added incentive not to use the telephone during electrical storms.

Why I don't remember the eerie sight escapes me, but when I stop and think about it, I probably don't remember it because I didn't see it. I was always scared half to death by a thunderstorm. I was probably hiding someplace like under the bed.

# 29. R. F. D. No. 1

The cheap, white paint soon faded away, leaving the bold black letters as dominant as ever. It was symbolic of government bungling. I suppose we will never completely rid ourselves of government waste and folly.

During the Roaring Twenties, our mail carrier drove up in front of our house in his Model T Ford roadster about noon six days a week, unless a blizzard had blocked the roads. Sometimes when the roads were blocked in places, he would make the first part of his route one day and reverse direction the next day, serving the end of the route first. He continued this procedure until the entire route was open.

Mail service was excellent. Each day, except Sunday, he delivered the daily newspaper on the day it was printed—even the early edition of the *Topeka Daily Capitol*, which was printed over a hundred miles away. On Monday we could mail an order to "Monkey" Wards or Sears Roebuck in Kansas City. The carrier picked up the order about noon, took it to town, and put it in the mail to Kansas City that evening. It caught the night train and was delivered to the mail-order house Tuesday morning. The order was filled that day, put in the mail that evening, caught the evening train, and arrived at our post office Wednesday morning. We received the merchandise Wednesday at noon, just forty-eight hours after we mailed the order. We counted on it, and if service was delayed for a day, we became concerned.

Postal employees took great pride in serving their customers. And mail-order houses plugged and honored their commitment to twenty-four hour service. Those same reliable services continued through the Depression.

Passenger trains were the fastest mode of transportation on most routes and were by far the safest and most reliable. Each train sported a railway express car immediately following the locomotive and tender. Aboard each express car was a railway mail clerk to handle the mail.

Every station where the train stopped had two mail drops—one at each end of the loading platform. The engineer stopped the train with the mail car next to the box in the direction the train was headed. The mail clerk collected the mail and sorted it on the way to the next station. If a letter went to the next town down the line, the clerk dropped it off and it made the next local delivery.

A post office at a small whistle-stop where passenger trains did not stop regularly received the same dedicated service. The postmaster or postmistress sacked the mail and took it to the railroad station. The station agent attached a large ring to the sack and hung it on a pole beside the track. As the train passed through, the mail clerk swung out a special hook to snatch the sack on the run. He kicked out the sacks of incoming mail for the station agent to pick up. This was the service we had at the small community where I attended high school and where about everyone knew both the station agent and the postmistress.

When you had some idea of the train schedules, you pretty well knew when a letter would be collected and delivered. You took it to the train station and dropped it in the proper box right up to the time the railway mail clerk opened the box. If the same train went to the letter's destination, you counted on the letter making the first delivery after the train arrived, even at distant cities. Service was less certain when post offices or mail clerks must transfer mail between railroads, but delays seldom exceeded one day.

Some other people could not count on service that fast—those living in or near towns not served by a railroad. Their mail was delivered to the nearest railroad stop and trucked to outlying post offices. But you counted on it making each transfer to the first available train or truck, keeping any delay to a minimum.

We heard talk of airmail, but most of us didn't trust those flimsy flying machines. Weather often delayed flights for a day or more, making surface mail faster anyway. Besides, an airmail stamp cost ten cents and first-class postage was just two cents.

The Sunday paper with the funnies was delivered on Monday, along with Monday's paper. For kids, comics were the best part of a paper. During the school year, we always hurried home on Mondays to get to this highlight of the week.

One time Mildred and I were playing—I guess it was post office—and put some things including a brick in the mailbox, forgetting to take them out. When the mail carrier found them, he let us know in no uncertain terms that he didn't like that and that the box was for mail only.

Our mailbox was the typical galvanized iron type with a rounded top. Dad originally put it on the side of the road next to the house. That made it on the carrier's left as he approached it. Then the postal service issued a regulation that required all mail boxes to be on the carrier's right side, so we moved it across the road. That seemed a little silly to us. Few cars traveled the road, and some days the mailman's Model T would be the only one. I suppose the regulation did have merit along well-traveled roads and highways.

I don't know how Dad had his name lettered on the box, but it looked professional in perfectly printed large, black, block letters. The regulation that took the cake was that all boxes had to be painted white with the name in black. If we didn't get it done within a specified time, it would be painted for us and we would be charged.

One day the carrier didn't come and he didn't come. We were worried. About four o'clock he showed up with a bucket of paint and a helper. They dabbed white paint over the box and then with a cloth wiped the paint off the letters already there, leaving the lettering somewhat smudged with white paint and fuzzy edges.

The cheap, white paint soon faded away, leaving the bold, black letters as dominant as ever. It remained a galvanized box with black lettering as long as we needed a mailbox.

# 30. Beans or Else

I hated beans. But it was eat them or go hungry. I ate. I learned to like.

Dad came from a long line of Pennsylvania Dutch who lived off the land on farms that were almost entirely self-sufficient. He inherited their self-reliance and the ability to tackle almost any task that befell him. He also learned the knack of providing as much of our livelihood as feasible right on the farm.

Every year we had a garden, although gardens on the windswept plains of Kansas generally were not overly productive. Tomatoes did poorly, but onions we raised in abundance—green ones early and dry ones to carry us well into the cold season. Green beans usually did well, often producing enough for canning. Early plantings of radishes and lettuce were excellent, but hot weather kept their season short.

When I was a wee lad, our garden was uphill from the well, and watering it was almost impossible. Later we moved it to the other side of the yard, downhill from the well, where we could water it easily. The move increased productivity.

Potatoes were a yearly crop. We bought seed potatoes and cut them in small pieces, making certain each piece had at least one eye. When the seed was all cut, Dad took a team and walking plow and started the patch with a furrow along one edge. The rest of the family—including me—walked along the furrow dropping the seeds in it. Then Dad plowed another furrow, covering up the planted spuds, and an additional furrow for spacing the rows. We kept repeating the process until all potatoes were in the ground.

In early summer, a job for Mildred or me or both was to go to the patch and dig new potatoes for dinner that day. We looked for the most mature-looking plants, expecting to find the best and biggest potatoes there.

Digging the crop in early fall was also a family affair. Dad or one of my older brothers drove the team and plowed up the potatoes one row at a time, and the rest of the family followed along and picked them up. After the first good rain, we went back and looked for potatoes we had missed during the initial harvest but which the rain had uncovered. We stored the potatoes in the cellar and had potatoes well into the winter.

## 30. Beans or Else

Some parts of Kansas produce excellent corn, but in the black soil of the windswept area where we lived, hot winds often burned the tassels before the ears were pollinated, and that often reduced the yield to near zero. It was not a good cash crop. Sweet corn matures earlier than field corn and quite often pollinates ahead of the hottest winds. It was more reliable and better for roasting ears. We always planted some corn, however, and even if it never produced much of a crop, we had roasting ears. We often cut the corn off the cobs and dried it in the sun to eat the next winter. That didn't always work too well. Bugs seemed to like the stuff better than we did.

One year we planted a fair-sized patch of pinto beans. They did great. When they were ripe and very dry, we gathered them, put them in an old trailer bed, and walked and stomped on them until all the beans were threshed out of their pods. We picked out the largest parts of the vines, but far too much chaff remained. Of course Dad knew what to do then. He winnowed them by taking a scoop full at a time, holding it high in the air, and letting the beans and chaff trickle off the end of the scoop. The Kansas wind blew most of the chaff away while the beans fell back in the trailer.

I was intrigued by the process but not by the thought of eating the things. I hated beans. And being the spoiled brat that I was, I usually managed to avoid them. But Kansas winters can be harsh and often change one's outlook, as was the case the following winter. Snow cascaded on the area, and the wind piled it into drifts that blocked all country roads until no one dared to get out and go to town. We were completely snowbound. Our supplies of most staples were soon exhausted, but we had homegrown pinto beans, homegrown onions, home canned tomatoes, and home-cured bacon.

I guess it was Mother's original recipe when she put them all together. I hated beans! But it was eat beans or go hungry. I ate. I learned to like them.

# 31. New Beds

Dad built our house when he and Mother were first married. It was adequate for our family with five bedrooms, three upstairs and two downstairs. Mom, Dad, and Mildred slept downstairs and we four boys, upstairs. The smallest of the upstairs rooms was a storeroom to put anything that we didn't have a better place for. That left two bedrooms for four boys. Two beds in each room made a place to sleep company, which we had from time to time. Each bed was equipped with wood slats, coil springs, and a tufted cotton mattress.

Each of us boys knew the route to our bed and could and usually did find our way without a light. We removed our shoes and socks downstairs. When we reached the bed, we peeled off our overalls, hung them on the bedpost, and piled into bed, sleeping in our everyday shirts. The exception was when we came home after we had dressed up and gone somewhere. Then we carried a coal oil lamp upstairs so we could see to put our good clothes away.

Each of these two upstairs rooms had two windows, and in the summer we always arranged the beds so that we had cross-ventilation, something we needed during hot Kansas summers. Sheets were all the cover we ever used, and sometimes we didn't need them. For the most part we had no heat in any of our bedrooms, so winter was a different story. We kept windows closed, piled on the covers, and slept between double blankets.

First it was an itch here and there—welts like chigger or mosquito bites. Then we discovered that we had little flat, red bugs crawling around on the upstairs beds. Except for color, these bugs looked much like wood ticks. Mother knew what they were—bedbugs. They raised welts when they bit. Fortunately, they never reached the downstairs bedrooms.

Now bedbugs were considered a sign of poor housekeeping and cast a stigma on anyone whose beds harbored them. Where we got them we weren't sure. Our favored fall guy was a hired hand. It helped to soften the stigma, and besides, he was no longer there to defend himself.

The war was on. One sure way to kill the varmints was to douse them with gasoline—if you could find them. Small leather tufts that held tucks in the mattresses provided excellent havens for the little pests, as did joints in the wooden

## 31. New Beds

bedsteads. Time and again Mother went over all the mattresses and bed frames, squirting gasoline into the joints and under the tufts. We felt no itch the next night after a treatment and thought we were rid of the bugs. It was only a matter of time until their return. Mother repeated and expanded the operation with gasoline to include all cracks around window frames and base boards. Still in time they returned, and each time they were worse until they became unbearable. The situation was desperate and called for drastic action.

First, we removed all the beds and bedding from the upstairs rooms since they contained most of the hiding and breeding places for the nasty insects. Then we followed with the gasoline treatment for all crevices in the woodwork. That removed the bugs from the house but left a problem of where to sleep. Before removing the beds, Mother had sewn up some mattress covers and we stuffed them with straw from the newest straw stacks to make straw ticks. We needed our bed linens so, on the day we removed the bed linens she gave them a thorough laundering with strong lye soap. The rest of the job was going to take a while, so we made our beds on the floor.

The mattresses were hopeless, so we burned them. We left springs lying for several days in the hot Kansas sun, which took care of them. We refinished all the wooden bedsteads and painted the iron ones. That filled all crevices and openings with paint or varnish.

After a matter of weeks or maybe months, we moved the bedsteads and springs back upstairs and placed the straw ticks on them. Our cash flow was not too good at the time, so new mattresses had to wait. We replaced them one at a time until eventually we were back in real beds again. Our nights had been almost like camping out, although we had no nighttime varmints pestering us in our sleep. We never knew a bed could feel so good.

# 32. Fast-Forward Farming

How many crops does one get off a piece of ground in one season? That depends on many factors.

When girls are too young to be of much help around the kitchen, they play house with tea sets, toy appliances, dolls, and the like. Sometimes when I didn't have a brother handy, I played house with Mildred. She didn't have a tea set, so we used pieces of discarded broken dishes. We laid our house out with stakes and binder twine; most of the furniture was make-believe. When it came to dolls, I drew the line. After all, tending the babies was a woman's job.

Boys often pattern their play after their father's vocation, so Forrest and I farmed under the fruit trees in our backyard. In the early 1920s, Ford Motor Company marketed toy models of their products—an effective method of advertising and promoting them. The toys were made of cast iron and, unlike most toys, they lasted what seemed like a lifetime. The folks bought me a Fordson tractor and Mildred a Model T coach. That model Ford was patterned somewhat like the old stagecoach in that it had the doors in the middle. The front had divided seats, and the front passengers got in the rear and wedged themselves between the front seats. Later, Forrest and I saved our pennies. He bought a Fordson tractor and I, a Model T truck. Mildred wasn't prone to play in the dirt with her car, so after the new wore off, she turned it over to me. I was really well-equipped with a car, tractor and truck.

When one of us didn't have a store-bought car, he made one out of a block of wood. Seats were wooden cleats nailed crosswise. A big nail made the steering wheel, smaller nails, the shifting lever and hand brake, and still smaller nails, the foot pedals. Add a little imagination and they ran fine.

We also made our farm implements. For a two-bottom lister, we took strips of thin, strap iron from the edge of the side boards of an old wagon bed, pointed and sharpened the ends, bent them into a "U" shape, and fastened them together with a crossbar. Put enough weight on the thing, and it made furrows as neat as you could want. Ridge busters came in a variety of shapes. To make a harrow, we drove many small brads through a thin block of wood with the points sticking down. It did a superb job of smoothing our fields. A disk was a spring about three-quarters of an inch diameter with the two ends tied by a wire, which held it in a curve. A larger and longer spring, left straight, was a drill for seeding the crop.

We inherited a threshing machine that Oscar and Lyle had built before Forrest and I began farming. It had many of the working parts of a real machine. Sides were decked out with pulleys, belts, and other components of a real thresher. The blower swiveled for stowing atop the machine in transit and extended while threshing. The blower housing was the bottom of a tin can. The feeder also folded for transit and extended for operating. The drive belt was a triple seam of an old pair of overalls. Although in real life a Fordson tractor was not hefty enough to pull a thresher, it did fine for us. After all, we didn't have a steam engine.

Forrest and I each had a set of imaginary improvements and had our own fields lain out between the trees. The layout was complete with graded roads from our houses to the little village. An old, long, box-like structure served as a line of shops.

Crops grew fast. We would list. Then we would bust the ridges. Then we'd disk, harrow, and sow our wheat. By the time we got the crop in, Mother would be calling us to dinner. By the time we had eaten and got back to the farm, wheat was ready to cut. How many crops did we raise in a summer? Your guess is as good as mine.

# 33. Butchering Time

At times we envied people living in town. They went to the grocery store and bought meat whenever they wished. Some even had iceboxes to keep it cool. But our way had some advantages, too. Our beef and pork was on the hoof and ready for the taking. The worst part was that meat spoils so fast in hot weather that we had fresh meat only in the winter. And best of all—especially during the Depression—we had no outlandish cash expenditures.

Beef was easier to butcher than pork. Dad and my older brothers set up a three-pole derrick with block and tackle, brought the animal in, shot it in the head, and hung it by the rear legs. Then they removed its hide, split it down the belly, and removed the insides, which included the heart, liver, and intestines. The rest was an anticlimax consisting of cutting up the carcass and cleaning up the mess.

And what did I do all this time? Being the smallest, I was errand boy. I fetched and delivered anything anyone needed. As soon as the liver was out, I carried it in to Mother. We always had liver on butchering day since it would spoil in a short time.

Consuming a large bull before some of it spoils could be a challenge for some, but our family of seven had little trouble. Sometimes we had an abundance of beef. If the weather seemed unfavorable for keeping it, we canned some, made corned beef, or did both. This way we could keep the beef well into hot weather.

Canning was Mother's job. She cooked the meat and sealed it in half-gallon jars. The canned meat was never quite as good as fresh meat, and occasionally a jar of it spoiled.

Making corned beef was Dad's job. He poured water in a twelve-gallon crock, put an unbroken egg in it, and started stirring in salt. When the brine became dense enough to float the egg, it was ready. I guess the cuts he used were mainly brisket, and he laid them in the crock and weighted them down to keep them submerged in the brine. We kept it in the crock, removing a little at a time as we used it.

## 33. Butchering Time

Butchering a hog involved more preparation. To be good for butchering, a hog had to be as fat as reasonably possible. The fat produced lard for cooking and making laundry soap.

We scalded the hog in a scalding vat—a flat wood trough large enough to lay the animal inside. The vat had sheet iron on the bottom to keep it from catching fire. We dug a trench for a fire pit, aligning and locating it so that the wind would provide draft and carry the smoke away. We hoped the wind didn't shift before the job was finished. We put the vat over the trench, filled it with water, and gathered wood for the fire. Who gathered the wood? The errand boy supplied a good portion of it.

When the water was hot, we "stuck the hog"—that is cut its throat. When it had bled to death, we placed it in the vat, and rolled it over to scald it so we could scrape the hair off easily. It was like wetting your beard to shave. About the only time I ever got to touch an animal during butchering was to help scrape hair off a hog.

When the hide was clean, we strung the hog up on the derrick. We didn't skin a hog. We cut up the carcass leaving the skin on. Again, I went directly to the kitchen with the liver for eating that day.

We trimmed out the fat and threw it into a large iron caldron for rendering. Then we built a fire under it, melted out the lard, and stored the rendered lard in lard cans that held about five gallons each.

Some small pieces, which were too small to be good for cooking, were saved out and ground into sausage. Sometimes if we wanted more sausage, we supplemented these pieces with larger cuts. One of Mother's jobs was to prepare the casings or turning the intestines inside out and cleaning them for stuffing the sausage. If we didn't have a stuffing machine or didn't have enough casings, we formed the sausage into patties. We put the sausage into lard cans and poured melted lard over it. When we wanted sausage to eat, we dug some out and covered the rest back up with lard. Submerged in the lard, the meat kept for weeks.

The good thing about pork is that, with the right care, more of it can be preserved well into the summer. We cured hams and bacon with salt, sugar, and smoke, and I believe some other preservatives. It kept well into hot weather, but if you wanted the ham to be the best, you boiled the salt out of it before cooking and eating. Fried bacon was always salty.

Dad always bought liquid smoke for curing, but many of our neighbors had smoke houses. A farmer with a smoke house hung his hams and bacon in it and built a fire inside. The process worked fine most of the time, but occasionally a smokehouse built of wood burned down and cooked the meat prematurely. The liquid smoke was better. I knew because Dad used it and Dad always knew best.

Butchering day was always a family affair. It brought us all together in a real team effort.

# 34. Static

Unless you had a phenomenal memory for numbers, you needed to write it down in the log. And what would happen if you didn't? Well, you might never find it again.

When Lyle and Oscar were in high school, they made friends with two brothers living in Pratt, who dabbled with radio and automobile electrical systems. One day in the mid-1920s, Lyle and Oscar brought home our first radio. It was a home-assembled set with earphones. It operated on an "A" battery and two forty-five volt "B" batteries as did all early radios, even when electrical service was available. The problem with using commercial electricity was an "AC hum"—the 60-cycle tone caused by alternating current.

The "A" battery was a six-volt battery, the same as a car battery. A "B" battery contained thirty dry cells, each cell the size of a flashlight battery and developing one-and-a-half volts.

Early sets needed elaborate aerials to pick up the broadcast signals and also had to be grounded. Lyle and Oscar erected a pole about twenty-five or thirty feet high and anchored it against the chicken house. Then they strung a braided copper wire aerial from the top of the pole to the house chimney. It was insulated at both ends. A lead in the same type of wire brought the signal down from the aerial through a window to the radio. An iron stake driven two or three feet into the ground, with a wire that connected to the radio, furnished the ground.

You can well imagine that the elaborate aerial had a powerful attraction for lightning, as much as or more than the windmill. When a thunderstorm approached, one of the first duties was disconnecting the antenna. Otherwise, it was goodbye radio. Connecting the antenna to the ground was a good idea, because that reduced the danger of unwanted electrical discharges entering the house.

The vacuum tube was the heart of radio, and all tubes were identical. Each tube had four prongs and fit into a standard socket. One tube was the detector and picked up the signal from the aerial. Additional tubes were amplifiers, each one amplifying the signal from the previous one. Thus, the more tubes you had, the louder and better the sound, so quality of a radio was judged primarily by the number of tubes; you had a three-tube, a five-tube, or maybe a powerful ten-tube set.

All early sets came with standardized jacks, for plugging in the speaker or earphones. Our radio came with earphones. We bought a gadget designed to go over an earphone and fit onto a grapherphone horn to make a speaker. It worked but was not very loud. Later we bought a real speaker. It was somewhat better than the improvised one, but at best, a three-tube set barely handled a speaker. You had to be close to the set to enjoy it. Earphones were better.

Many sets had more than one tuning dial, and some had as many as three. Our three-tube set had one dial and a control that tapped on to a series of "buttons." Dials on the earliest radios did not identify frequencies of broadcasting stations. You might even find the same station on more than one setting of the dials.

Since controls on the set did not identify frequencies, you had to hunt. Standard operating procedure required a radio log by the set. When you found a station, you listened until they announced their call letters and then recorded the call letters and dial settings on the log. Next time you wanted that station, you knew where to set your dials.

As you zeroed onto a station, you heard squealing and squawking. If you were not interested in the radio, the noise could "drive you up the wall." Static was also a perpetual problem. It was especially bad when thunderstorms were around, even if they were a hundred miles or more away.

But radio technology advanced rapidly. After about two years with our little set, Lyle brought home an Atwater Kent five-tube set borrowed from his friend. I think his friend dreamed of making a profit by selling it to us. It had a single tuning dial and handled the speaker beautifully; Mother fell in love with it. She never tried to tune the old set, but this one was easy to tune and she really enjoyed it. But the dial did not identify frequencies. We still had to keep a log. The sad part was that we couldn't keep it.

# 35. Sonny Boy

I can still picture him on his knee with his hand reaching upward, singing with such compassion in his strong and melodious voice. It's a memory to last a lifetime.

During the early Roaring Twenties, movie theaters ran shows six days a week. They were a popular pastime on Friday and Saturday. That was especially true for farmers, who seldom got to town during the week. Before the main feature, they usually showed a news clip and maybe a short subject. Then came the customary comedy, followed by the main feature. Some of the dialogue you guessed at, but for the parts that were difficult to interpret, the picture was interrupted and the words flashed on the screen.

Each theater showed three shows a day—an afternoon matinee and a first and second show in the evening. The doors did not close during a show, so you could go in at any time during the show. Moviegoers often entered in the middle of a show and sat through the entire second showing. We were not great movie fans, so getting to see a picture show was a real treat.

The Kansas Theater in Pratt showed second-string movies. In the mid-1920s, it was getting rather dilapidated and run down, so the owners remodeled and modernized it. The grand opening sounded enticing, so much so that we couldn't resist. We five kids drove into town the opening night, bought our tickets and sat down to enjoy the show.

At this grand opening, however, just before the main feature, they came in with a western movie. Oh well, we sat and enjoyed it. We weren't far into the western when it got real exciting. Just as everybody's attention climaxed at high pitch, the picture abruptly stopped and the screen read:

## "Continued next week"

Of course we all wanted to know what happened next.

Those show people were clever. Since the busiest days for the movies were Friday and Saturday, they held their grand opening early in the week, hoping to draw a huge crowd. Then they started the serial western, hoping to continue the larger turnouts early in each following week.

We fell for their trick, but we couldn't all go every week. It cost a lot, and sometimes some of us had other things to do. So each week, either Lyle or Oscar drove and took one or two of us little ones to see a chapter. When we got home, we told the story to the rest so that nobody lost out on the saga. It lasted about ten weeks.

The first-run theater across the street was more sophisticated. It had an orchestra pit in front of the screen and an orchestra that furnished music and sound effects for the movie. Shortly after the dramatic western serial, two classic first-run movies came to the town. One was a movie rendition of *Ben Hur* and the other, *The Big Parade*. *Ben Hur* was a little over my head. However, I had no trouble with *The Big Parade*.

The setting for *The Big Parade* was the World War. It pictured buddies from their induction through training into battle in France. Dad went along. His hearing and eyesight were getting poor, so we sat down front, close to the orchestra pit. The sound effects were great. The rumble of tanks, the whining of Flying Jennies, and the cracking of rifles all seemed so real.

However, when our men reached the battlefield, things got hairy. They were dodging bullets from strafing aircraft, taking rifle bullets, and dying on the battlefield. Blood oozed from under their helmets. The sound of rifles and cannons was deafening. I had about all I could take by the middle of the late show. About that time, the orchestra had put in their time, so they turned off the sound, picked up their instruments and went home. I truly welcomed the silence.

After these two classics, it was time to remodel the big theater. They renamed it *The Barron*. And guess what? The pictures talked—no more reading the lines. And something else, the place was now air-conditioned—no more sticking to your seat in hot weather.

Again we attended the opening show, *The Singing Fool*, starring Al Jolson. And what a show it was. I can still picture Jolson on his knee with his hand reaching upward, singing "Sonny Boy" with compassion in his strong and melodious voice as only Jolson could.

# 36. The Runaway

Forrest caught up to the scene. We hitched the horses back to the cultivator and returned to the cornfield where I resumed my training as though nothing unusual had happened.

The midsummer day was warm and sunny and the corn was ready to cultivate. I was about ten years old and grown up enough to earnestly begin fieldwork on the farm. Forrest was my tutor. I harnessed the horses, although I was barely strong enough and tall enough to manhandle the harness and lift it to the horses' backs. I hitched the team to the cultivator and headed the mile or so down the road to the cornfield with Forrest walking behind in his coaching position.

As anyone who has run a horse-drawn cultivator in the field knows, the machine had to be steered from side to side by the rider to keep from plowing up the crop and still get the weeds close to it. I had already been indoctrinated on guiding the apparatus. Our cultivator had a gadget that locked the gangs of shovels to keep them from swaying back and forth when they were out of the ground. It moved steadily down the road like a cart, and I felt secure in the seat.

Our horses were getting old and lazy, and I lacked the experience to keep them moving at the proper pace. Forrest, in his desire to speed them up, heaved some small clods at their rumps to get them going. It worked.

After a quick squat, they took off down the road at full gallop with me in tow. I yanked on the reins to no avail. Stopping them that way was like trying to hold back a freight train with your bare hands. Now, I had heard stories of how to curb a runaway team by steering them into the side ditch, so I tried it. By the time one horse reached the shoulder of the road, the cultivator wheel went into the ditch. The locking gadget came loose and the machine swerved sideways, catching the gang in the wheel. When that gang started up and down beside my ear, I quickly got the mares back in the road. By this time we were well past our cornfield and swaying back and forth toward my uncle's house.

His house had a long driveway that headed straight toward his front door until making an "S" shaped curve to the side of it. The driveway was not graded but had two dirt tracks about twelve inches wide and four or five inches deep with a grassy median between. It was smooth riding if you stayed in the tracks but otherwise it was more than a little rough.

My runaway team elected to go up that driveway. They stayed in the tracks but the cultivator didn't. That's where the water jug and I parted company with the cultivator, and I watched it scramble up the driveway and out of sight around the curve. I got to my feet and made my way around the curve into Uncle Sam's yard. There was my uncle, unhitching the horses where they finally stopped. They had made the first part of the S-curve but missed the second, left the drive, and straddled a small tree. The cultivator rested on top of the tree.

Several minutes later, Forrest arrived on the scene. The three of us got the cultivator off the tree. We hitched the team back to the cultivator and returned to the cornfield where I resumed my training. The lesson I learned best that day was "don't throw clods at horses when they don't expect it."

# 37. Organs

At the beginning of the century, few people owned pianos; the pump organ was much more popular. We had one that was very ornate with a mirror and lots of carving and gingerbread. It must have stood six or seven feet high. The make was Windsor—"Monkey" Ward's trade name. Mother played it some, but we had no real musicians in the family.

Two foot pedals connected to bellows supplied air to activate the reeds—one reed for each key on the keyboard. Actually the thing had three bellows. One was connected to each pedal, and it pumped air into a master bellows so as to keep an even supply of air. That's different from an accordion, which only sounds when you move the bellows.

You had two ways to control volume. One way was with stops above the keys and the other with knee pedals. Other stops provided various tones and effects. Our organ had a total of eleven stops.

Mildred and I took piano lessons for a few summers when school was not in session, but we practiced on the organ. The two are not the same. Neither of us became very good. Later, after we quit taking lessons, I picked up my own method of playing a melody with my right hand and cording with the left. I entertained myself, but few others.

As the instrument aged, some or the reeds lost their tone quality, and straps that connected the foot pedals to the bellows wore out. When one of the straps broke, I replaced it with an old leather belt. When I removed the front panels from the organ, I could see ends of the reeds.

When one note failed to respond at all, I again removed the front panels. Each reed had a slot in the end, so I could insert a hook and pull it out. I quickly found the faulty reed and removed it. It was really cruddy, so I cleaned and replaced it. Then it sounded good as new—better than some other notes. Why not clean all the reeds? I did that, and the organ sounded like a different instrument.

Uncle Elmo and Aunt Inez also had a nice organ, but it was not quite as ornate as ours. Uncle Elmo could play it and could sing quite well—at least to us non-musicians it sounded good. Union Valley School had an organ. Uncle Elmo was our schoolmaster for two sessions, and he taught us music and also played the organ.

My uncle later moved his family to town but kept and worked the farm. Their organ was getting old, so they left it behind in the farmhouse. We were helping him harvest one summer and stayed in the old house. One day the rains came, and we couldn't cut wheat.

The old organ was not working, so I had another chance to use my experience repairing an organ. I replaced a bellows strap and cleaned all the reeds. The old organ worked as good as new. But my uncle didn't sing the old song we used to think was so funny.

The song was about Arkansas and didn't picture it as much of a place. In part, it went:

"…I got so thin on sassafras tea I could hide behind a straw. If I ever see that land again, it'll be through a telescope from here to Arkansas."

After a woman from Arkansas was so upset she became nauseated, he never sang the song again.

# 38. Bigots

When I was in the fifth grade, our headmaster was a local young man not dedicated to a career of teaching—at least not in elementary school. The school board decided to hire an experienced teacher for the following year, so when Grace McAnarney applied, they hired her on the spot. Grace was a woman who had a family and had spent several years in the classroom. The board had found a "gold mine."

So they thought, until someone learned the new teacher was Catholic. That didn't bother me, but Mother and other board members were aware of the quirks, biases, and bigotries of people. Although the board was happy with its choice, they thought it best to ask Mrs. McAnarney to surrender her contract. But she did what any responsible citizen would have done. She refused. It was too late for her to land another contract.

The hiring of Grace McAnarney also caused tension within some families—mainly the Brehm families. Dave Brehm was a blacksmith in Pratt. He had two brothers, Jake and Andy, who farmed in the Union Valley School District. Jake had a son, Fred, who was in my class. Andy was dedicated to the community and served many consecutive terms on the school board, although his offspring had long since gone through elementary school. He was serving on the board while Mother was secretary.

Several families pulled their children out of the school and transported them to neighboring schools rather than have them subjected to teaching by a Catholic. Fred Brehm from my class was one of the kids made to surrender his loyalty.

Apparently, the situation caused a rift between the Brehm brothers, because Andy helped hire the teacher and stood behind the choice. The following spring at the annual school meeting, Andy was nominated for another term on the board. He declined. Who could blame him?

Rumors permeated the district that some of Grace's behavior was rather odd. Most of them were as far-fetched and ridiculous as some dreamed up by political candidates. One was that she had shot a man. Although most intelligent adults took the rumors for what they were, when school opened, many of us in the schoolroom felt some apprehension—you might say we were scared.

I think Grace sensed the tension and soon laid it to rest. Children from one family attending Union Valley had difficulty in learning, and most of them left school when they reached the age of sixteen without completing the eighth grade. One of them, Cleve, was a large, muscular guy pushing the age of sixteen. He sat at one of the largest desks at the very back of the room. He was a prince of a fellow but one you wouldn't want to cross. One day soon after school opened in the fall, Grace came walking down the aisle and asked, "Does someone have a ruler I can borrow?"

We were all ready to oblige, but I got the honor. Then she said, "I've got a score to settle with Cleve."

Cleve turned red, and now things were really tense. We could visualize Cleve making mincemeat out of Grace. That was until she started rapping him gently on the shoulder and counting the strokes. We recalled that it was his sixteenth birthday. He turned redder than ever but by then it was no longer fear, I guess you would call it embarrassment.

Later she laughed at the story of her shooting at a man, and I believe her story. They once had a chicken house in their yard, and one night she heard a commotion in it. Someone was stealing chickens. She got a handgun, opened the window, and yelled, "Get out of that chicken house." Then she fired two shots in the air and one in the ground. The thieves left in a hurry. The next day the McAnarneys repaired chicken roosts that the invaders had not bothered to go over, under, or around.

Grace lived at home in Pratt and rode horseback to and from school, quartering her horse in the barn during the school day. While riding, she wore loose, black bloomers—the kind worn by female athletes of the day. On a few occasions we stayed after school while she prepared to return home. She hid behind the stove to don her bloomers.

Each morning we recited the Pledge of Allegiance and repeated the Lord's Prayer. The ending of the Catholic version of the prayer differs slightly from the Protestant version. Grace remained graciously and reverently silent while we said our final words. As sure as we were in the classroom, no one ever pressed any religious beliefs on another. America truly meant religious freedom.

Those of us who remained loyal to Union Valley grew to love our teacher, and she and her husband remained friends of our family long after the school year was over. As the year drew to a close, all of the students got together and agreed to put in a dime each to buy our teacher a going away present. Mildred and I drew the honor of buying the gift. You couldn't get much for a dollar, but we shopped and shopped. Finally, we settled for a nice, small vase.

We elected Harrison Dean, the older of the two black boys, to present the gift. He made a splendid presentation and we all agreed when he wound it up saying, "We're giving this gift to the best teacher we ever had." Tears welled in her eyes.

# 39. Back to the Farm

By the time Lyle finished the eighth grade, he was old enough to take on much of the farmwork, so he put off high school for a year, and Dad took back the rented portion of the farm. Since we didn't have enough horses left to work all the land, Dad bought a tractor and a few farm implements to pull behind it. At the time, many farmers insisted that tractors were not practical and would never take the place of horses, but Dad had faith. To buy the new equipment, he put an even higher mortgage on the place. But we got to keep all the wheat and any other crops we grew.

Oscar finished grade school the next year and took Lyle's place working the farm. We bought a second-hand Model T touring car, and Lyle drove it to and from high school in Pratt.

Forrest was two years behind Oscar, so Oscar stayed out of high school until mid-term of the second year. The next year Forrest stayed out of school to work the farm. Oscar finished high school in three-and-a-half years and still graduated one year behind Lyle.

But by the time Lyle had finished high school, the burden of the farm mortgage overwhelmed us. Dad was forced to sell the farm, but bought another smaller, less expensive one in the western part of the county. We moved in the summer of 1928.

# 40. Turkey Shoot

Turkey was a rare treat at our house. In fact, I don't believe we had ever had a turkey for Thanksgiving or Christmas dinner until the year I went on a "turkey shoot."

We always celebrated each Thanksgiving and Christmas with a family get together. Thanksgiving was spent with Uncle Elmo and Aunt Inez, Mother's sister, and her family who lived on a farm about six miles from us. Christmas brought three families together—the same two along with the family of Uncle Elmer, Mother's brother who was an engineer for the Rock Island Railroad.

One Saturday in November, the Pratt Chamber of Commerce sponsored a turkey hunt as a business promotion. The hunt was open to students no further along in school than the eighth grade. I was in the eighth grade at the top of the eligibility list.

At eleven o'clock on that Saturday, each participating merchant was supposed to place a letter of the alphabet in the window. The challenge to contestants was to walk the streets and identify the merchants who displayed the letters spelling, "A Merry Christmas." Each of the first ten kids to get back to the municipal building with a correct listing won a live turkey. The letters were black on green cards about four inches square.

Pratt was not a large town, and most businesses were within two blocks of the main intersection. A few were up north, where the Rock Island Railroad crossed Main Street. Still Pratt had many more businesses than "A Merry Christmas" had letters, so some stores displayed other letters that showed they also were cooperating in the event.

I was never a fast one on something of this nature, but I was game to try. I found several of the letters in short order. When I came to an "X," I wondered whether they tricked us with "Xmas." No, they wouldn't do that—not with so many letters to display. One "R" was very elusive. Several of us got a ride in the back of a truck up to the railroad tracks to look for letters. Some contestants would sight a letter that, to me, was not in the same format, so I ignored it.

After an hour I finally put down the name of a merchant displaying a monogrammed "R" and headed for the municipal building. I didn't have much hope since by that time the line extended well into the street. However, one by one the contestants were turned away disappointed.

Eventually, I was about tenth in line when my cousin came by and whispered in my ear, "J.C. Penney forgot to put their $R$ in the window until just now."

He had been in their store when someone checking the entries had sent a representative to find out why Penney's had never appeared on any entry. Minutes later I won the first turkey. In line a few places behind me was a brother to the cousin who had tipped me off. He won the second turkey. We had my cousin's turkey for Thanksgiving dinner, and I fattened mine for Christmas.

# 41. No More Log

If we waited too long, we had to crank the car by hand. That was no great problem because the battery was soon charged back to normal.

By the time we moved to our new farm near Cullison, the single dial radio had just about taken over the market. A few three-dial sets were still available and were "selling for a song." We latched onto a three-dial, five-tube set that served us well for several years.

Radio had advanced considerably by the early 1930s. The "B" battery eliminator came into use, so if you had 110-volt electric service, you no longer needed "B" batteries. More advanced vacuum tubes also made the scene by the early 1930s, and the all electric set came into being as did the dials that identified frequencies. By then each station came in at a certain position of the dial. You no longer needed to keep a station log.

Also, in the 1930s, for farmers without electricity, the one battery set came on the market. It used the "A" battery only which was identical to six-volt car battery. You used the two interchangeably. When the battery ran down on the radio, you could swap batteries between your car and radio, letting the car charge up the rundown battery. But if you drained the battery too low on the radio, then you had to crank the car by hand. Of course, once you get the car running, it quickly recharged the battery. Wind chargers also came onto the market.

In the mid-1930s, Oscar bought an up-to-date Zenith radio that operated on the "A" battery only. He got hold of instructions for building a wind charger using an automobile generator. He carved the propeller out of a one-by-four piece of lumber and bolted it to the generator. He built the tower from old scrap angle iron and mounted it on top of the workshop. It worked great. We had two batteries, swapping them frequently from charger to radio—really "uptown."

# 42. Sittin' in the Rain

In our rural area, everyday wear for male high school students was bib overalls. For special events, we dressed as best we could.

We at Cullison High School were fortunate in such a small school to have a high-caliber superintendent and principal, Mr. Brown. He was an all right guy and sported a white Essex roadster with a rumble seat.

Our basketball team always played in the state tournament, often taking first. We had football for four years, but that's a different story. Where we really starred was in academics.

The state administered scholarship tests every year in several cities, and Cullison High usually brought home several medals. We went to Dodge City for the exams my freshman year. I was competing in English and general science.

We all dressed up in our Sunday best. I had outgrown my earlier dress clothes, so for the occasion, Mother and Dad bought me a new wool suit with two pairs of pants. Granted it was cheap, but when new, it looked quite snazzy.

Students, faculty, and parents furnished transportation by private automobiles. On that beautiful, sunny spring morning, we made it to Dodge City without a hitch. We took some exams before noon, had the rare treat of eating lunch in a restaurant, and finished our tests by mid-afternoon. We were really pumped up when the exams were over, and another student and I persuaded Mr. Brown to let us ride back in the rumble seat of his Essex. We were only a few miles out of Dodge City when we saw a huge thundercloud approaching us head-on.

Mr. Brown put the throttle to the floor. Before the storm hit, he overtook one of the students who was driving an old Buick sedan and hauling three other students. That made six of us not too uncomfortable, and we were in out of the rain or so we thought.

Roofs on sedans of that vintage were composed of wood slats covered with chicken wire, padding, and waterproof fabric similar to that used on open models. But we hadn't seen rain for some time. Dry weather had taken its toll. The fabric was checked and cracked and was no longer waterproof.

When the rain hit, it was a genuine cloudburst like so many Great Plains thunderstorms. The roof offered a little protection, like maybe sitting under a sieve. The headliner and cushions became water logged as did all our clothes. Water continued to fall on us, even after we were out of the shower and in the sunshine.

What happened to my new suit? Wool fabric and water are not compatible. When I got home, the suit fit like a corset, much tighter than last year's clothes. But at least I still had one pair of pants that fit.

By the next spring, we really felt the pinch of the Depression. I had no new suit to wear to Dodge City, but I did have a nice pair of trousers. Out of necessity, dress was more casual.

# 43. Westward Bound

When pioneers opened up the West, they faced an unknown future as they moved to new territory. Times hadn't entirely changed by the late 1920s.

In spite of our financial difficulties when we moved to the western part of the county in 1928, for most people, the economy was booming—it still was the Roaring Twenties. Farmers and investors were buying up land in Eastern Colorado as though there would be no more. Colorado weather was unusually good during the latter part of the decade, and some farmers did well raising wheat there.

As the West was opening up, Dad had moved west throughout his lifetime, and he couldn't resist the temptation to buy some of the rich Colorado land.

He mortgaged the new farm and signed the contract for Colorado land just about the time the stock market crashed in 1929. And as if that weren't bad enough, the great drought began shortly thereafter. Lyle and Oscar put in one crop of wheat that didn't produce enough to harvest. The following spring, Oscar and I drove to Colorado in the old Model T and put out a crop of maize. It didn't even come up.

By this time the dust bowl had begun in earnest, and our land was right in the middle of it. The drought and dust forced us to abandon the land, and by that time it was no longer marketable, because nobody wanted it.

And even worse, the mortgage on the home place was eating us up. Our Realtor took over our mortgage and rented the farm to us for a few years. We managed to hang on for a while in spite of falling wheat prices and virtually no outside source of income. But the farm no longer belonged to us.

Nobody knows what tragedy or triumph lie ahead. We live one day at a time.

# 44. Business as Usual

She drove past our house two or three times a week just as her husband had been doing. Things hadn't changed noticeably except for the gender of the driver.

Some optimistic entrepreneur built the eight-story Roberts Hotel in Pratt about the time the stock market crashed in 1929. It was truly the finest in town. Business was good during the first few years of operation.

Shortly after Franklin Delano Roosevelt became president in 1933, he managed to get the eighteenth amendment repealed, putting Al Capone and Elliot Ness out of business. But Kansas and Oklahoma didn't see fit to repeal their bans on liquor and remained dry, at least on the books.

Money was scarce during those years, and most farmers struggled to make ends meet. But Mr. Brotman, our neighbor who lived a few miles down the road, seemed to do fairly well in spite of the poor sandy soil that made up his farm. He passed our house several times a week delivering milk to the Roberts Hotel. But if he had a dairy, he kept his cows hidden. Nobody ever saw them.

He carried his milk into the hotel in cases of white milk bottles, as you would expect. The odd thing was that when he brought the empties out, the bottles were still white. Word got around.

Just what he was delivering we never knew. We weren't his customers. But rotgut whiskey and white lightning no longer were run of the mill. Bootleggers hauled in bonded liquor from neighboring states and sold it at huge profits. The only bad thing was that one had to take what was available—he had little choice.

Not many people were bothered about it. Prohibition was no longer a national issue and had limited support locally. To a few people, however, the law was the law, and liquor was bad. These few raised enough of a stink that the sheriff thought it advisable to pay Mr. Brotman a visit.

Pratt is not a large town and just about everyone knew, or at least recognized, the sheriff. We knew it was the sheriff when he passed our house and headed toward Brotman's farm. When he returned, Mr. Brotman was in the car with him. Brotman spent a few weeks as the sheriff's guest in the county jail.

It was during those few weeks when Mr. Brotman was away, that Mrs. Brotman drove past our house delivering the milk to the hotel. When he returned, nothing changed. It was and had been business as usual.

# 45. Chips

The chips burned. I presume they heated the house, but I didn't need a fire to keep warm.

By the early 1930s, we were feeling the ever-increasing pinch of the Depression as it leveled its wrath on the country. Coal had become less expensive, but cash to buy it was almost nonexistent, so we began looking for alternate fuels. Wood sounded good, but few trees remained to be cut in our section of Kansas. We had to haul our wood six to ten miles. Nevertheless, we used less cash to buy gas for the truck than to buy coal, so we cut wood. Cottonwood was most plentiful, but it burned fast. Hackberry was quite good. Some other woods were in between, but the traditional oak and pecan trees were very scarce.

On one unusually warm winter day at about one o'clock in the afternoon, our school superintendent came into the classroom and relayed to us a cold wave warning. The Rock Island station agent had received the alert by way of his company telegraph and relayed it to the school. The south wind was strong, and dust reduced visibility to less than a mile sometimes. The day set a record warm temperature.

That evening I had just finished the chores and was in the hayloft. It was about dark when the wind subsided considerably and then suddenly shifted to the north. The first gust hit so hard I could feel the barn give. Returning to the house, I had to fight a strong Blue Norther and could feel the temperature drop even during the brief time I took to make the short trip.

By this time Forrest and I alternated the chore of building fires, relieving Mother from the grueling chore. The next day was my morning to rise early. I first built a fire in the dining room, which was on the north side of the house. I had the stove red hot, but the room was still frigid. We had broken a north basement window, and it was letting the wind in. The north wind was so strong that it came up through the single flooring and lifted the linoleum rug off the floor. I gave up on that room, closed the door into the kitchen, and built a fire in the kitchen range. We lived in the kitchen until the wind subsided that evening. The next morning set a record cold temperature following the record warm temperature the day before. School was canceled.

Once we ran out of both wood and coal with no way to get either in short order. Mother had lived through hard times in the gay nineties and remembered that they had burned cow chips. Could it be? Yes. And who gathered the chips? Although I was a teenager by this time, I was still the youngest. The chips burned and I presume they heated the house. I didn't need a fire to keep warm. The chips burned so fast that I kept warm running from pasture to house to supply fuel to warm the rest of the family.

# 46. Four Wheels—No Brakes

Some early automobiles provided real excitement. The amazing thing is that we are here to talk about it.

Automobiles, from their invention through the mid-1920s, traveled slowly and stopped with relative ease, but the brakes left a lot to be desired. The Model T Ford had a single brake drum in the transmission, but conventional brakes on most cars were on the rear wheels. Brake drums were fitted with external bands exposed to the weather. They wore down rapidly under any conditions but were especially vulnerable on our muddy country roads. One trip to town after a rain, and we needed to adjust the bands. After two trips, we needed to replace them. By 1928, all new cars featured four-wheel brakes, but several years passed before all the oldies with poor brakes were retired to the junk heap.

High-pressure tires, three to four inches in diameter, graced the early Model T and other early cars. Most of these tires were clinchers—that is the tire had beads that fitted into grooves in a rim mounted permanently to the wheel. When a tire went flat—a common occurrence—you had two choices. You could repair the tire on the spot, or you could drive on to your destination on the flat tire. You could drive quite some distance on a flat clincher without ruining the tire.

Just about every motorist carried a jack, tire irons, a tube patching kit, and a tire pump. When a tire went flat, you jacked up the wheel and removed the tire from the rim. Then you removed the tube from the tire, buffed the tube around the hole, fitted a patch, applied cement, and stuck down the patch. Then you replaced the tube and tire, pumped it up, removed the jack, and you were ready to go. A spare tire helped, but still you had to remove the flat from the rim, mount the spare, and pump it up by hand.

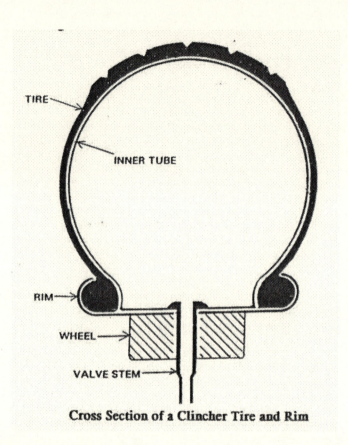

**Cross Section of a Clincher Tire and Rim**

A few cars used straight side tires on removable rims. Although the clincher had enough stretch to let you get one edge over the rim, straight side tires had wire beads that had no stretch, so designers came out with a variety of rims that let the tire off the rim with no stretching. The removable rims permitted the carrying of a mounted, inflated spare. When equipped with straight side tires, you no longer needed to carry a tire pump.

The balloon tire introduced in the mid-1920s soon became standard on all cars including the last two years of the Model T Ford, 1926–27. In 1928, the Model A Ford hit the market with welded wire wheels and four-wheel brakes as standard equipment. A drop center rim was part of the wheel. Your spare was mounted on a spare wheel. When you had a flat, you changed the whole wheel. The new rim revolutionized wheel design and became standard on all cars by the early 1930s.

## 46. Four Wheels—No Brakes

I know no end to the uses of a used inner tube. Strips of rubber cut from it were the propellant for a homemade slingshot. A cross-cut section of the tube made an excellent heavy-duty rubber band, the desired strength determined by the width of the band. When melted down, the rubber made an effective non-slip dressing for a drive belt or a temporary patch for some leak. On our new farm, we had a gravity flow pump that would not force as much water through a garden hose as it pumped. I kept our garden watered by connecting joints of old two-inch well casing with sections of old inner tubes. It worked well, but moving it around was more than a little cumbersome.

We were driving the old 1925 Chevrolet truck and Essex touring car when I was learning to drive. Later we acquired a Chevy touring car of the same vintage as our truck. I learned to drive with four wheels and no brakes, so defensive driving was an essential part of my training. Slow down early and be alert for an escape route.

In the little village of Cullison, no one worried about parking on the left side of the street. I was driving into the town one morning and swung across the street to stop facing another car. It had rained the day before, and I failed to allow for the debilitating effect it had on my brakes. When I realized I had to do something to avoid hitting the car, I steered into a tree. At the creeping speed, damage to the car was very minor and damage to the tree was nil.

By the time I was sixteen, the harvester-thresher combine had pretty well replaced the stationary thresher. I had the responsibility of hauling wheat from the machine to the elevator. With time of the essence and with four wheels and no brakes, driving a loaded truck was hair-raising indeed. Usually the approach to scales at an elevator was uphill, and stopping a loaded truck with no brakes on the level scales, without running off the other end, took some careful maneuvering.

At one elevator, the drive from scales to the dump was also uphill. On one late evening trip, I killed the engine on this climb. No brakes left me coasting backward, so I put the thing in reverse—a mistake. It ripped a gear in the transmission, and then I had no low speed or reverse. One rear wheel ended up in a hole beside the scales. I had the scales blocked, and no way could I climb out, starting with the transmission in second gear. When a Good Samaritan arrived with a load of wheat, he chained me to his truck and snatched me out of the hole. I started the load to one side downhill, circled the scale house, crossed the scales, and made the dump. The trip home, using only second and third gears, was a cinch. We always had spare parts for the Chevys, so the next morning we replaced the stripped gear and were back to cutting wheat almost as early as usual.

Some early cars were slow to perfect joints in the linkage between their steering gears and front wheels. Our Chevys used ball-and-socket joints, which wore rather rapidly—especially if not greased frequently. Worn joints were prone to dropping a steering rod when you least expected, leaving the driver with no steering control.

High winds in a thunderstorm one night blew down our windmill. Lyle and Oscar spotted a used steel tower and took the truck to haul it home. A twenty-five-foot tower on a truck bed, five feet by eight feet, makes a very insecure load. On the way home, the truck dropped a steering rod and took to the side ditch. They not only had to reconnect the steering rod but also had to reload the tower.

A frequent and spontaneous get-together following a marriage, was the charivari. One night we had the old Chevy touring car loaded with kids on the way to charivari a couple. We were sneaking up on them with our lights out when the car dropped a steering rod and rolled off the road into the ditch. We got out, cut a rubber band from an old inner tube, replaced the rod, secured it with the rubber band, and drove on to the party. Rubber bands worked fine for the job if replaced frequently, but grease from the joint caused the rubber to deteriorate.

The most amazing thing is that we all lived to look back on those days and shiver to think of what might have been.

# 47. The Government Helped

Some have said, "We look to the government for a solution when government is the problem." Has that been truth or fiction?

During the early 1930s, the Depression got worse each year, and prices for goods and services dropped well below what they were in the Roaring Twenties. Farmers produced lots of wheat—more than they had a market for—and the price dropped so low that, although other prices were down, wheat farmers could rarely break even.

Then the government offered a program designed to help. In order to reduce the production of wheat, the government paid farmers to let a third of their land lie idle each year and grow a crop on that third the following year. This was a practice known as summer fallowing, and one that was not new to most wheat farmers. During the year it is idle, the land stores moisture and nutrients, and the process is especially effective during a drought such as the one we were in.

As a result, the first summer-fallowed crop yielded twice as much as before, and we had a greater surplus than ever. The price of wheat dropped to twenty-five cents a bushel. Typical of so many government programs, this one only compounded the problem it was designed to solve.

But the government kept trying, and the next program was to reduce acreage even more. A farmer was to plow up some of his crop or use it for pasture without harvesting it. For doing this, he received an "allotment"—a government subsidy for not farming. During the drought, much of the crop dried up or the wind blew the dry, dusty topsoil away, leaving no wheat anyway. This was the part of the crop that the farmers "destroyed."

But Uncle Sam did provide some relief. To determine acreages under cultivation and destroyed, the government established a measuring technique using a simple device for measuring angles and a big wheel that was one rod around. The wheel operator rolled the wheel along each edge of a field or patch and counted the revolutions. He measured the angles formed by the sides. He then sent the measurements to the county agent who figured acreages. Many destitute farmers—including the Snyders—took on the job of measuring fields to provide a little cash flow when things were tight. And of course, the county offices made jobs for others.

So what happened? That program also backfired. Many farmers were tenants on land owned by others, many of whom were bankers. Since the farmers received the allotments, some land owners—even some bankers—took over the job of farming, even though they had no farm equipment and often knew little about the business of farming. They then hired their former tenants to work the farm at a starvation price per acre and collected the allotments themselves. The program dealt a death blow to many of those farmers whom it was designed to help.

But government aid was not for farmers alone. The Works Progress Administration (WPA) put many people on the government's payroll. The going wage for non-skilled labor was twenty-five cents an hour. But our generous politicians set a minimum wage of forty cents. In those days, most people looked on the WPA as relief, and they preferred working rather than going on relief. So if they could find jobs, most industrious workers took them at twenty-five cents an hour while WPA workers leaned on their shovels at forty cents an hour.

But we can't overlook genuine help of government for the genuinely destitute. The soup lines of the 1930s are legendary. They were the sole source of nutrition for some. Farmers generally were more fortunate than those in the soup lines since most had their own milk and eggs, butter, chickens, beef, and pork. A good garden also helped.

Still one has to wonder, "How fast would the economy have recovered if government had left it strictly to the law of supply and demand?" We'll never know. But we do know that the New Deal programs cost lots of tax dollars, and many of them accomplished little, or even worse, they failed by increasing the problems they were created to solve.

# 48. Stop, Look, Listen

The street was closed, so we turned around, and left for home. We could get our chicken feed another day.

Mother needed to go to Pratt that hot summer afternoon to do some shopping. It was shortly after harvest, and my older brothers were busy on the farm, so I inherited the privilege of driving her in our old Chevy touring car. One of the items we needed was chicken feed, which we usually bought at the Wheat Belt Hatchery. Mother was loyal to them because they had been good to her.

When the hatchery first opened, the proprietor set up a contest to name his establishment. He offered a flock of baby chicks to the winner. Mother entered the name "Wheat Belt Hatchery," and that is the name he chose. The disappointing part is that two other people—almost as smart as Mother—thought of the same name, so she received only one third of a flock.

After making our other purchases, we headed out to find the hatchery. It had moved to the west part of town since the last time we had been there. We drove west to the street we thought we wanted and turned north until we came to the Rock Island Railroad track. Mother said, "Stop," and I, being the obedient son, stopped.

But about a half block east was the rear end of a freight train, so I said to Mother, "There won't be any trains coming with that train stopped there." My Uncle Elmer, the engineer on the Rock Island Railroad, had related many facts and tales about the railroad. I thought then that I knew a lot about railroading.

Normally, a freight train hitched a caboose on the rear of the train. The conductor and rear brakeman had a cupola atop a genuine caboose from which they could see the entire train.

Since it was so soon after harvest, the railroads serving the wheat belt were running many extra trains to move the grain, so many trains in fact, that they didn't have enough cabooses to go around. When no caboose was available, they dug up an old, mothballed wooden passenger coach to serve instead. During the many years that these old coaches sat on sidings, they had accumulated an abundance of soot and dust, and the wood had lost much of its structural integrity. Since the coach had no cupola, to improve visibility, the train pulled an empty tank car directly in front of the coach. This was true for the one on the track a half block east.

We proceeded north but failed to find the chicken place, so we turned back south coming again to the railroad track. Mother repeated her warning, "Stop."

I did, but again said, "Mother, there won't be any trains."

We didn't give up on finding the hatchery. We turned around and headed north coming to the tracks for a third time, and again Mother said, "Stop."

Before I had time to reply, I was glad I had stopped. Rumbling down the track was this giant locomotive pulling a string of freight cars at about thirty miles per hour. I had heard of train wrecks before, and my first reaction was that when the trains collided, the rear train might buckle and the boxcars fall on top of us. I jammed the car in reverse and promptly killed the engine.

I looked down the track, and a number of people were scattering on both sides of the temporary caboose; what so many people were doing in the car I have no idea. The engineer hit the ground just before contact, and I presume the fireman did the same on the opposite side.

The crash was something to behold. Flying soot, dust, glass, and wood made a dark "fog" that blocked our view of everything beyond. When the air cleared, we saw one car where two had been. The tanker had a canopy resembling the top of an old wooden passenger coach and had double the usual number of trucks underneath.

I don't remember hearing a whistle as the train approached. That's probably because there wasn't one. When the engine passed in front of us, the engineer was on the lowest step prepared to jump and probably was already there when he passed the whistle point.

No one was hurt, but my uncle told us later that the engineer was exceeding the yard speed limit and that he had been involved in accidents before and probably was through as an engineer.

But now the street was closed, so we turned around, and left for home. We could get our chicken feed another day.

# 49. Skip to My Lou

Life for teenagers on the farm was not all work and no play. A favorite pastime in the summer was the yard party. And we especially favored it during the Depression because it was inexpensive. It required no formal invitations, no elaborate garb, no planning other than date and place, and no cash outlay beyond a few refreshments by the host. Everybody was welcome. You just let a few people know you are planning a party, and the grapevine got going.

The best time for a party was during a full moon. Few farms had electricity for lighting. But with a full moon, who needed lights? On rare occasions, we lighted the yard by car headlights, but that often led to dead batteries and is not recommended.

We all knew quite a repertoire of games, and changing from game to game was spontaneous. "Skip to my Lou" was a favorite. Somebody led off the singing and the way we went in a circle swinging our partners at the end of each verse and taking a new partner for the next one:

"Skip, skip, skip to my Lou,
Skip, skip, skip to my Lou,
Skip, skip, skip to my Lou,
Skip to my Lou, my darlin.'

Oh, I'll get another one better than you,
I'll get another one better than you,
I'll get another one better than you,
Skip to my Lou, my darlin.'"

And more.

A few minutes of that and then it was another favorite, "Miller Boy." The routine of singing and swinging was much the same, but to a different tune and lyrics:

"Happy is the miller boy who lives by the mill,
The mill goes round with a right good will,
One hand in the hopper and the other in the sack,
Ladies step forward and the gents fall back."

And on to the next verse.

These were just two of many, but they all provided ample opportunity for the boys to take the girls in their arms and swing them around. It was great fun.

The party began about twilight and continued on until ten or eleven o'clock. Then the host or host's parents served refreshments, which were usually cookies and lemonade or cake. If the host felt generous, he or she might even serve ice cream.

Many grown-ups frowned on the idea of young folks petting and necking, although most of them did at times. And I'll bet our parents were not a lot different in their younger days. But at our yard parties, boys and girls were in each other's arms, and no one thought of it as necking or petting, only as wholesome fun.

# 50. Tin Lizzy

You get up, dust yourself off, and get back to the job at hand. Injuries are not serious, but the embarrassment is something else.

For some reason, people associate tin with being cheap. Actually, tin is a rather expensive metal. Henry Ford is known for putting America on wheels. To do so, early in the twentieth century, he established the assembly line and built his cars at significantly less cost than his competition could. He also pioneered the five dollar-a-day wage, thus demonstrating to the world that employee-management cooperation is the best solution for promoting efficient production and profitable business.

He built the first Model T Ford sometime around 1910, and kept it in production with occasional updating through 1927. You could buy one for considerably less than any competitive make, hence the connotation of cheap and the label of "Tin Lizzy."

Model T Ford coupe, circa 1923–1925

Bashing of and bragging about Ford and its competitors were the subjects of many discussions and arguments, which sometimes became heated. Which automobile was best in the mud? Which was safest? Which rode the best? Which was most dependable? Which was easiest to maintain and work on?

The Model T had a number of features that were unique for the day. One was its transmission, which used planetary gears and bands while the competition stayed with the manual changing of gears. On the Model T, you had a lever to the left of the driver and three floor pedals. Throttle and spark controls were just below the steering wheel, with the throttle on the right and spark on the left.

The left pedal was the clutch, the low-gear pedal, the middle, the reverse pedal, and the right, the brake. All the way back, the lever disengaged the clutch and transmission and applied parking brakes on the rear wheels, although the parking brakes were usually worn until they were ineffective. Full forward, the lever put you in high gear—that is unless you held the left pedal down slightly, which disengaged the clutch and took it out of gear. To go forward, you pulled down the throttle to give a little gas and put the low pedal all the way to the floor while putting the lever forward. When you got rolling, you let up on the throttle and pedal and went into high gear. To back up, you held the low-clutch pedal down slightly, to keep it out of high gear, and put the center pedal all the way down.

The brake band was in the transmission, so the differential left the rear wheels free to rotate in opposite directions when you applied the brake. Often when one wheel was on a dry surface and the other on a slick surface, such as mud or ice, you would see the dizzy phenomenon of the dry wheel running forward and the slick one spinning backward.

If you didn't keep your brake band tight and your brakes were poor, you had a backup. If you needed to stop in a hurry, you used the reverse pedal. Since this did not involve any direct meshing of gears, you did no damage. However, the procedure was not recommended.

Ford's competition used the six-volt storage battery introduced in the early years of the century while the Model T used a magneto. The self-starter, which ran from the battery, was a big selling feature for the competition, so Henry made starter and battery available as an option. That gave him a great advantage. If your battery went dead, as it frequently did, you fell back on the magneto.

Of course, to start the engine with a magneto, you had to crank it by hand. A crank on the front end was standard on all Model Ts. Also, to make starting easier, the Model T had a choke control out front. The crank hung down where you could bend it if you straddled some high obstacle, so often the Tin Lizzy owner mounted a strap up front to hang the crank high enough to avoid any hazards.

Another feature unique to the Tin Lizzy was its ignition system. If you are in the dark as to the purpose of a coil on a car, it transforms the low battery or magneto voltage to high voltage for creating a spark, which ignites the fuel mixture in the engine. You had two circuits: the primary six-volt magneto or battery circuit and the secondary high-voltage circuit. The conventional car had one coil and distributed the high voltage to the cylinders. The Model T distributed the low voltage to four coils, one for each cylinder. When the coil failed in a conventional car, you were stranded. When a coil went bad on the Model T, you limped home on three cylinders. The spark control either advanced or delayed the time the engine fired. When the engine was turning slowly, as during cranking, an advanced spark could fire the engine too soon, turning it backward—"kick" was the word. When it kicked, it could sprain your wrist, or if the crank came out of your hand, it could come around and whack the back of your wrist. Either was true discomfort, so you wanted never to forget to retard the spark before cranking. Once the engine was running, advancing the spark improved power and performance. To get the maximum speed, you "pulled the ears together." This meant pulling both spark and throttle levers all the way down.

Tin Lizzy coils became an exciting tool for practical jokers. You could use one on any vehicle—it didn't have to be a Tin Lizzy. Connect the low-voltage primary circuit to a six-volt hot wire and ground it to any metal part of the car, but put a switch in the circuit to deactivate the device until the switch is closed. Then, connect the secondary high-voltage terminal to the car body and the other to a chain hanging to the ground. Rubber tires prevented completion of the circuit—that is until somebody standing on the ground touched the car. Wow! Low amperage prevented any injury, but the high-voltage shock was quite disturbing and a little uncomfortable.

Another crazy feature was construction of the magneto. On most electric generators, the armature turns inside a rigid field. But on the Model T, the armature was flat and mounted on the back of the engine, while the field was attached to the rear end of the crankshaft and was part of the flywheel. Rotating relative to each other generated an electric current.

When a Tin Lizzy was new, everything fit tight. You turned the crank, the magneto did its job, and the engine started. But engines did wear, developing end play of the crankshaft. This endplay allowed the field and armature of the magneto to separate enough, so that at cranking speed it did not generate sufficient current to fire the spark plugs. But when in high gear, pressure of the clutch face on the rear of the crankshaft forced it forward, bringing the field and armature together. But how do you stand up front and crank the thing when it's in high gear? Simple—you jack up a rear wheel. Try it a few times and you learn a few things. When the engine kicks off and the car starts bucking, it quite likely will come off the jack. So always block a wheel so the thing won't move. And what if you don't? Well, a Model T doesn't weigh much. When it rolls over you, injuries, if any, are slight. You get up, dust yourself off, go find your old Tin Lizzy, and get back to the job at hand.

# 51. The Champ?

When I'm feeling low, I take a look at it. It's always good for a laugh.

Talent is something that some people have and others don't. When it comes to athletics, I don't. I guess I'm not the world's most poorly coordinated individual, but in a contest to find him, I'd probably make the finals. Occasionally, during my first seven years at Union Valley, we would choose up sides for pumpkin ball or some other game. The pumpkin ball was like a softball, except that it had outer seams. As a first-grade student, I expected to be the last one chosen. By the time I reached the second grade, first graders were chosen ahead of me. In the third grade, it was both first and second graders. And so it went on through the seventh grade. I still was the last one chosen.

The high school I attended introduced football for the first time during my sophomore year. The school never had more than about sixty-five or seventy students. Assuming half were male, you can readily see that putting together twenty-two men for first and second football teams took all talent available, and some of the players showed little skill.

Forrest, a senior that year, went out for football and talked me into joining him. He thought it would do me good. Forrest made the first team, but as one might suspect, I didn't. No doubt it was good for my physique but did nothing to inflate my ego.

Our center was a real bruiser, towering to nearly six feet and weighing well over two hundred pounds. To block the center on most high school defenses, all he had to do was be there. The chance of his being injured and taken out of the game was extremely unlikely, so who filled the slot on the second team? I, the least talented, filled the spot. Faith in our center was justified, because I was never sent in as a substitute.

But I did have my moments. Our coach was high on intramural sports and went all out to give everyone a chance to compete. He organized a football game between a team of seventh and eighth graders and our high school second team. I played center throughout the entire game. We won. Quite possibly our training and knowledge of the game helped us while our opponents had virtually no formal coaching. Besides that, we were somewhat larger and heavier than they were.

That same year we also held an intramural track meet, and again I starred. I came in second in the half-mile and first in the mile, which made me high point man in the junior class. Apparently, what I lacked in skill I made up in stamina.

After graduation, several members of my class returned for post-graduate courses, because no jobs were available and few of us could afford college. At the end of basketball season, we had an intramural tournament. The seventh and eighth grades, each high school class, and the faculty entered teams.

But since the faculty had only three men, the coach, the grade school coach, and the superintendent, they had to borrow some. These came from the graduates, including me.

I played forward. At one point, our coach came dribbling down the center of the court while I charged down the right side. He passed the ball to me and I was supposed to pass it back to him under the goal. The problem was that he had five players guarding him, and no way could I get the ball through them. But since I was wide open and close to the net, I took a shot and made us two points. Some people just don't learn. Later, in an almost exact repeat of the first play when I hit the basket, I raised my game total to four points. The faculty won the tournament.

Our school joker kept score. After the game he told me in a voice loud enough for all to hear, "When you made your first basket, I made the score so big I didn't have room for the second score."

The school gave me a certificate that reads, "…has received this certificate of award as intramural champion in basketball." I have it framed and hanging in my den. When I'm feeling low, I take a look at it. It's always good for a laugh.

# 52. Are We Really Farming?

During the Depression, you worked at whatever you could find. It was better than starving.

The summer I finished my fifth year of high school, our real estate agent could no longer hang on to the farm. He, too, had undergone foreclosure. We were forced to move. The owner of a farm near Haviland had retired a few years earlier and sold his farm to a neighboring farmer, carrying the mortgage himself. When the buyer couldn't hack it, the owner was forced to foreclose.

When he took back his farm, he did what many other land owners were doing; he elected to farm it himself but hire someone to work it by the acre. That way he collected the allotment—the government handout supposed to help the farmer. He rented the improvements to us, giving us a place to live. It was the best we could find, so we ceased for the time to be farmers. We were just tenants and hired workers.

He was cheap. Not only did he pay a very minimum rate for the work, but he did minimum tilling, not preparing the land properly. He then wondered why we didn't raise better crops for him.

We hung on. It was rough. Since we moved in August, we had no garden, and the summer was too far gone to plant one. For the first few months, we didn't get all we would have liked to eat, although we didn't exactly go hungry. We did have chickens and eggs.

But we were in the middle of the Depression, and you worked at whatever you could find. It's better than starving.

# 53. A Broken Heart

"Don't let them do anything to my fingernails." That was her request as she lay there, filing and polishing her nails.

Students in our school lived on farms or in Cullison, a town of only a few hundred people. The Depression was at its peak, and few young people could find jobs when finishing high school, much less could afford college. It wasn't uncommon for the young people to marry a year or so after graduation from high school.

Violet, a lovely girl, graduated in my class. She was not overly popular with the opposite sex but had dated a few local boys while in high school. A year of so after graduation, I heard she had married a man from a neighboring town.

One hot August afternoon following my fifth year of high school, I received a shocking call from Violet's family. They wanted some of Violet's classmates to be pallbearers at her funeral.

As the story unfolded, we learned that she had undergone a hysterectomy and failed to recover. Her doctors said the surgery was entirely successful and could give no medical reason for her failure to survive. She had contracted syphilis or gonorrhea from her husband, and those venereal diseases had no known cure, other than removal of all diseased tissue.

Virginity was a virtue. Brides were expected to conform. Many men lived by a double standard, but most brides hoped the men were "clean" too. Venereal disease was a disgrace.

Apparently the shame, the humiliation, the disappointment in her husband, and the inability to have a normal family life were more than Violet could bear. She had lost her will to live. Lying in her hospital bed, filing and polishing her nails, she made her request, "Don't let them do anything to my fingernails."

The afternoon was torrid. Everyone agreed that we pallbearers should not wear the customary coats but wear light, starched cotton trousers, white shirts, and dark ties. Even these became drenched, in spite of having all church windows and doors open.

Not one of us could stifle the tears when we passed by her as she lay there on her sateen bed, her beautiful nails gleaming. This lovely young woman—dead of a broken heart.

# 54. Poisoned to Life

The poor sow was skinny as a rail, but she made it. We were glad that she had pulled through. The time was late August, just after we moved to Haviland.

One government program to ease the sting of the Depression was the Civilian Conservation Corps, the CCC, and one of their largest projects was planting shelter belts. A shelter belt is a strip of several rows of differing varieties of trees, and usually it is planted along the north side of an east-west road. Its purpose was to break the winter wind and hold the snow back from blocking the road.

The owner of the farm where we were working had ceded land to the government for them to plant a shelter belt, but it ran east-west through the middle of his farm rather than along a road. That spring the CCC had planted the trees.

Now as any Kansas farmer can tell you, you don't plant trees in that part of Kansas unless you have some way to keep them watered, especially in the middle of a drought. But nobody told the government, so as is typical of so many government programs, more of our taxes went down the drain. Maybe it had merit in that it kept some young men busy when they had nothing better to do.

When we moved in, we put our hogs in a pen fenced with hog wire. We had one sow that was getting old for a brood sow, so we had her fattened up to butcher when the weather cooled off. Now the farmer who preceded us had done a poor job of maintaining the hog pen fence, so our sow found her way under it and strayed out to the shelter belt looking for something different to eat.

Jackrabbits and cottontails thrived during the drought, and they ate what meager crops farmers raised. Because they also fed on the young trees the CCC had planted, the CCC spread poison bran throughout the belt in a futile effort to save the trees. And that bran is what our hog found to eat.

She managed to stagger home before the poison really hit her. When we found her, we thought she was gone for good. But Dad had been around farm animals all his life and poison was not new to him. He forced raw eggs and skim milk and who knows what else down her. She was panting for breath and wringing wet with sweat, but she was still alive. After a few hours she had thrown off the poison; she breathed more easily and finally got to her feet.

But the poison had taken its toll. She was skinny as a rail and no longer ready to butcher. Dad elected to let her raise another litter of pigs. Poison had saved her life.

# 55. An Affair with Whiskey

I loved my "Whiskey," and parting brought tears. Giving up "Whiskey" was like losing a longtime friend.

Drought spread throughout the high plains of the western Great Plains, the intermountain regions, and the desert Southwest. The drought compounded hardships of the Depression. Day after day, week after week, month after month, we stared at the sky praying for rain. It didn't come. Occasionally, a cloud towered upward giving some hope only to evaporate after no more than a sprinkle, if that. We were lucky to get fifteen bushels of wheat per acre when in normal and wet years an acre yielded from twenty-five to forty bushels.

In the fall of 1934, adequate rain in our section of Kansas brought some relief by wheat seeding time. Farmers got their wheat in early when the moisture was good, and we had some of the most lush, green wheat one could ever wish to see. It did so well that we were afraid it would joint before cold weather, and that meant probable winter kill.

Across the vast grazing lands of New Mexico and Arizona, cattle ranchers were not so lucky. Pastures were so dry that their cattle and horses were starving. If only their livestock could get to the green wheat pastures in Kansas, they could slow the rapid growth of the wheat, saving it from winter kill and, at the same time, saving the animals.

So, come they did. Ranchers shipped their starving cattle by the trainload and parceled them out to farmers for pasturing. Most Kansas wheat fields were unfenced, which meant that cattle had to be herded, so the ranchers shipped a few bony range horses along with the cattle.

One problem for some farmers was the lack of hay, straw, or some other form of dry bulk grass or hay to go along with the green wheat. Without the dry stuff, cattle would founder and die. The farm we were working was a natural. It was a section of land with a sand draw across the middle. A rather broad expanse of pasture meandered along each side of the draw where land was marginal for farming. Since we had only a few head of cattle ourselves, the pasture grew tall enough to produce the necessary dry bulk—no hay to buy or haul. Our landlord contracted for a hundred head of cattle and a horse, and he hired us to tend them.

## 55. An Affair with Whiskey

Forrest borrowed a saddle from a neighbor and went to the railroad yard to get the cattle and horse. When it arrived at our farm, that poor horse could hardly put one foot in front of the other. Every move it made was an effort. The horse was so skinny you could count its ribs from a hundred paces. The cattle were no better.

We had a small patch of wheat that was fenced, so we first put the cattle and horse there and only needed to move them to the pasture once or twice a day until they gained a little strength. Since we had no saddle of our own, we rented one from a nearby ranch that put on a rodeo every year. The saddle was a type used for riding bucking broncos, and in ordinary use you didn't need to be a horseman to stay in it. It held you like a suction cup.

By the time that first wheat patch was cut down to size, the horse's ribs had disappeared. He was alert and seemed ready to go. Forrest saddled him and mounted. Spirited he was as he reared up on his hind legs, and that's the time we appreciated that saddle, but that was the end of the show. From then on it was all business, and I took over most of the herding.

The first day out the cattle seemed content to feed on wheat pasture for an hour or two while "Whiskey" (that was my horse's name) and I lounged around, enjoying the warm autumn sun. But then the cattle got full and began to wander. One heifer took off for parts unknown and Whiskey and I took after. I did my best to get Whiskey to go around the heifer and cut her off from in front, but he turned only his head sideways and headed straight for the heifer. He won out and brought her right back into the herd. I knew then that when it came to cutting cattle, I didn't have horse sense.

Although old Whiskey seemed able enough on the job, sometimes when bending down to graze or get a drink, his knees bucked a little. He never fell, but I was always a little concerned.

One evening about milking time, I herded the cattle back into the pasture and decided to drive our milk cows to the barn. Our cows didn't know what a horse was, and they panicked. One of our prize milk cows took off in the wrong direction and headed straight for a washout in the draw, about four feet deep and eight feet across. Whiskey took chase and no way could I hold him. I doubted that our cow could jump the ditch and was certain that Whiskey would meet disaster while taking me with him. I froze in the saddle. In one graceful leap, the cow jumped the hazard with Whiskey in trail. When he jumped, I was still frozen. He had no problem clearing the ditch, but in my stiffened state, I went higher than he did. And when I was coming down, he was already coming up on his next jump. Oh, that hurt! After a few seconds I realized that my crotch extended no higher than before, and that I suffered no permanent injury. As a rider I gained a lot more faith in and respect for my steed. I'm certain that Whiskey didn't feel same about the rider.

Sometimes, in-between herding stints, Whiskey and I went for outings. He really liked to run and I shared his enthusiasm. We became buddies. But it seems all good things come to an end. Cattle went to the slaughterhouse and, although I don't really know, I assume poor Whiskey went to the glue factory. For a while I felt lost without Whiskey.

# 56. Rabbits

By the time we retired Whiskey in the fall of 1934, winter had set in. And at that time of year, wheat farmers had little to do other than the usual barnyard chores of tending chickens and livestock and taking care of milk.

Lyle had married and moved onto a farm of his own. Forrest also married and was working a full-time job in town. Dad was getting old, so for the most part, Oscar was now in charge of the home.

Some distant cousins of ours ran an upholstering and furniture repair shop in Winfield, Kansas. When it dawned on them that we were virtually idle, they suggested Oscar come to Winfield in January and help them for a few months. He couldn't very well get away and suggested I go instead. They decided to give me a try, and that's where I developed a love of furniture and established a hobby of woodworking.

Later in the spring, our cousins loaded me in their car and came to visit my family. The visit developed into a rare experience for them.

The drought was still on and for the most part crops were meager. But the dry weather was fine for breeding rabbits, so much so that their expanding population was eating far too much of the meager crops. What to do about it? You hold community rabbit drives.

Someone was always ready to spearhead a drive. He passed the word around, and the grapevine spread the message rapidly. Before a drive began, the sponsors went ahead and prepared a trap at the windup spot. They made a spiral pen from snow fencing with an opening on one side for the rabbits to enter.

Our neighborhood had planned a drive for the weekend we were there, and although country folks generally did the drives, our city cousins were game and joined in. The drive was scheduled to begin at two o'clock and covered an area two miles square. The day was as beautiful as a spring day can be.

People came from miles around and lined up around the edges of a four square mile area. One of the organizers drove the perimeter and spaced the people so as to leave equal distance between each two. Absolutely no guns were permitted, but everyone carried a club.

At two o'clock sharp, we started walking toward the center where the trap was in place. When we stirred up a rabbit early in the drive, it ran from us rather than escaping between the two of us. It's a good thing the rabbits weren't smart, because running between two of us at that stage would have been a cinch.

As we approached the center and the spacing between people became less and less, the odds of a rabbit's escape through the line decreased dramatically. Usually, someone could club the rabbit before it got away. A few rabbits made it. Cottontails were good eating, so often when somebody clubbed one of them, he held onto it and took it home for supper.

By the time we were within a quarter mile or so of the trap, people were shoulder to shoulder. The rabbits had little chance of escape. By this time, a few people needed to drop out. I was one who dropped out, because I couldn't stand the blood or take part in the massacre.

Those on the open side of the trap held back while those on the other side herded the victims around to the open side and into the pen. They closed the gate, climbed in, and clubbed the rabbits to death. The pile of rabbits was about three feet high and ten or twelve feet across. Farmers culled out the cottontails to eat and fed the jackrabbits to their hogs.

# 57. The Turkey Roost

When they coaxed me into gunning my truck, I expected to surprise everybody in the pit. However, no one was more surprised than I when the thing climbed over the bank and out of the pit. After that, loaders had little to say.

Pavement in our part of the country was restricted to city streets and a few miles of major highways out of the largest cities. But if you put enough sand and gravel on a road and work it into the top few inches of soil, you have a road that stands up in most weather. Most main highways and county roads were graveled and maintained so that you could drive them with little trouble in rain or shine.

But on country roads maintained by townships, mud continued to be a problem—especially for the mail carrier and school bus drivers who had to cope with them in all kinds of weather.

Most of our part of Kansas was good, black farmland lying on top of layers of sand. Ravines had cut into the black soil down to the sand, leaving the area laced with ribbons of sand we called sand draws. Local pools formed in the draws and filled with sand sometimes to a depth of four to six feet. Sand was close and plentiful.

Our township took advantage of the sand and did what we could with our share of county tax money. Township trustees were unsalaried. Most of the money went to maintaining and sanding rural roads. Priority for sanding went first to school bus routes, then to mail routes, and finally to providing every farmhome a graveled route to a highway.

Twice each year—in the spring before harvest and in the fall, after the wheat was in the ground—we put on a community "sanding bee." Most farmers had trucks and built sand beds for them. A sand bed had a trap door at the bottom for dumping the load at a destination. When sanding time came, farmers removed their grain beds and put on their sand beds.

The project called for more men than just the truck drivers, and all were from the township. One of the elected trustees served as supervisor and timekeeper at the sand pit. He paid himself by the hour as he did the other men. Another man out on the road supervised the unloading and tallied the loads dumped by each trucker. Men loaded the trucks with shovels. Wages were twenty-five cents an hour until the late 1930s, when they increased to thirty-five cents an hour.

A deep pool with four to six feet of sand provided an ideal location for getting gravel. After taking out a few loads, we had a pit with a high bank at the back about the same height as the top of a truck bed.

The driver backed his truck into the pit under its own power. As it neared the bank at the back, he gunned the engine so that it dug the rear wheels into the sand lowering the bed and, along with the high bank, making it easier to load.

Motor vehicles generally do not perform well in loose sand, especially loaded trucks. A local farmer with a four-horse team or a Caterpillar tractor snapped the loaded trucks out of the pit. From there, the trucker was left on his own.

Trucks were all makes and sizes. Some did better than others in the sand while others were better on the road. We were driving the old 1925 Chevy, which had small auto tires in front and thirty-five inch diameter tires on the rear. The truck looked as though it were always going downhill. The high wheels made the back of our bed the highest in the fleet, and it was dubbed the "Turkey Roost." Those large tires were a good thing at times, because they did not bury in loose ground or sand as fast as smaller tires.

During a sanding bee, I usually was on the end of a shovel and Oscar drove the truck. But one day Oscar had other pressing matters, and I drove the truck. When I backed into the pit, loaders griped because I didn't bury the wheels. "Gun it when you back in," they said.

Next time I did, but the little motor in our old Chevy lacked power to dig the high wheels into the sand. I expected to surprise everybody in the pit, but no one was more surprised than I when the thing climbed over the bank and out of the pit. After that, loaders resigned themselves to shoveling a little higher.

# 58. Stranded

During the Depression, you did what you could to help others and accepted help in return when you needed it. I feared that Oscar might not approve of what I was doing. After all, it was his car. But what the heck, when a "feller" needs a friend, you oblige.

It was a late summer afternoon. I was alone in Pratt, driving Oscar's Essex, and I stopped in at a service station where we knew the owner. I do not recall why I was alone in town or why I stopped at the station.

But inside was a long-faced guy who looked as though he might be in his 20s. I soon learned that he was from Medicine Lodge, about thirty miles from Pratt, and he needed to get home but was broke. He was a musician who had lost his job.

He was clean and neat. He was wearing no shirt but had a towel draped around his neck. My guess was that he had pawned all he could, including his shirt, to get as far as he had, but no one mentioned that subject. Hitchhiking was out of the question without a shirt and with darkness falling.

He asked if I could take him home. If I would get him to Medicine Lodge, he would get money from his dad and fill my tank with gas—not a bad deal if he made good on his promise. He had been at the station for a while and the owner vouched for him, so off we went. The road to Medicine Lodge was full of curves winding around the hills. Driving the curves was fun and a diversion from driving the monotonous straight roads in our flat country.

We made it to his home, but nobody was there. Small towns where everybody knows about everybody else are great. The musician had me drive him to a station where he and his dad were customers. Service stations did not normally sell on credit, but the station attendent filled my tank and charged it to the guy's dad. I was on my way home.

My concern about Oscar's disapproval was unfounded. He told me I had done a very humane thing, so I felt good about it.

# 59. The Hobo

Hitchhiking was sometimes a dependable means of transportation. Experience at it helped.

An important point to remember when "riding your thumb" was that standing was usually better than walking because, first, a passing driver got a better look at you, and second, you chose someplace where he had to slow down anyway and could stop more easily. A suitcase was important too. It helped to keep you from looking like a bum. And most importantly, dress neatly and try to be identified as a college student—a college sticker on the suitcase helped.

By the late 1920s, the harvester thresher combine had for the most part replaced the stationary thresher. We had our grain laid by much earlier, started our fall plowing sooner, and got on with other things.

In the summer of 1938, we hired two harvest hands, Jay and Clyde, from Missouri to help us harvest. After we were through with our landlord's crop, the two hired hands and I decided to follow the harvest. Wheat matures later and later the farther north and northwest you travel, so it wasn't many miles to standing wheat.

Jay had a Graham Paige sedan, about seven years old, which was our transportation. Sedans of that vintage had flat running boards along the sides. Accessories were available for carrying stuff. One was a trunk that bolted on behind, thus moving the spare tire further back. Another was a luggage rack that clamped to the outside edge of the running board. Our transport sported the latter.

We rolled up one of our three-quarter size mattresses and threw it in the back to defray the cost of room and board when we weren't working. All three of us rode up front.

The old Graham was not in the best of condition. However, it did do a phenomenal thirty miles on a gallon of gas and did almost that good on oil. It did use oil, lots of it, and we needed an ample supply.

Jay planned ahead. Because harvesting was a dusty job, we changed oil in our tractor and combine engines frequently—usually every other day. Jay rounded up several square five-gallon cans and saved the oil we drained from the machines. The cans lined up nicely on the running board inside the luggage rack. After every fifty miles or so, Jay got out and added oil from one of the cans, never bothering to check the level.

The first night out we reached Southern Nebraska. Clyde and I unrolled the mattress in a stubble field and Jay slept in the Graham. The next day, as we neared the southeast corner of the Nebraska Panhandle, Julesburg, Colorado, was only a few miles away. Jay and Clyde had never been in Colorado, so nothing would do but to drive into Julesburg and rent a cabin for the night.

The next day we drove north to Gurley, Nebraska, where we arrived about noon. Harvest was just starting. The three of us found work for about a day shocking bundles but had hoped for something that would last longer. That evening we drove to an elevator in Gurley to inquire about work. The proprietor hired me on the spot. We stayed with the car that night. Jay and Clyde returned to finish the shocking next day with my luggage still in the car. I was to find a place for room and board, and they were supposed to come into town that night to check on more work.

Now they had never been to Wyoming, either, and Cheyenne was not far away. After they finished shocking, they headed for Cheyenne with my luggage in tow. I waited for them at the town's one cafe—the only place open after dark. They hadn't shown up by closing time, and I was out in the cold.

I had heard of hobos sleeping in boxcars, so I headed for the tracks near the elevator. Typical of high altitudes, the Nebraska Panhandle gets cold at night, even in mid-summer. A boxcar is no place to spend the night. After a brief try at it, I looked for something better. Nearby was an auto graveyard, and there I found an old Essex coupe with all windows still in place. Compared to a boxcar, the one-seated coupe was quite cozy.

The next night Jay and Clyde showed up with my suitcase. They had stopped along the road, straddled a ditch and tightened the rods in the Graham. They decided they had enough of the harvest. They shipped our mattress home and headed for Missouri. I stayed on at the elevator until combining was over. Without transportation, I didn't look forward to moving farther north.

Four farmers in the area jointly owned a thresher and had bound some of their wheat. Each farmer furnished a team and bundle rack, and jointly they hired two spike pitchers who stayed in the field and helped load the bundle racks. I landed the job on one of the bundle racks and stayed at that farmer's place.

His wheat was the first we threshed, and he chose to fill his barn loft with straw before stacking the rest of it. He was the least affluent of the four, and his team was not made up of choice horses. His house was large enough for only his family, so I slept on the grain in the back of his truck parked in the barn the first night. Under freshly threshed straw is no place to sleep either. Beards sifting through the loft floor brought on itching and a rash like I had never known. The rest of the time we parked the truck under the stars in God's great outdoors.

When first starting a load, the bundle hauler ties the lines to the rack, dismounts, and helps pitch bundles. Farm horses are trained to walk along the shock row, so all the driving the hauler does while loading is, "Giddy up" and "Whoa." After the rack is about a third full, he has to be on the rack and load the bundles. The old nags I had were slow—too slow to please Geek, one of the spike pitchers. Once while I was still off the rack, to speed the horses up he prodded one in the rump with his pitchfork. They moved! One lunge and the neck yoke came off the tongue and the coupling pin came out, leaving them hitched only to the double tree. The more it hit them in the heels the harder they ran. Threshing stopped while the crew rounded up my team. The team was well-behaved after that. No one seemed to think the runaway resulted from my mishandling, so when Geek begged that I tell no one about the pitchfork, the incident remained our secret for the rest of the harvest.

When that job was finished, Geek and I joined two other transient farm hands to help another farmer and his son run their own small thresher, which they pulled with a John Deere tractor. I didn't present myself as an expert horseman, but one of the transients did. So I drove their team of mules and the other hand drove their team of prize horses. After demonstrating our skills in horsemanship, the farmer confided in me that he wished he had given me the horses instead of the mules.

We would all go to the field and load the racks. Then they cranked the John Deere, threshed the two loads, shut down the machine, and repeated the operation. The spike pitchers also helped unload the bundles from the racks into the thresher.

By the time that job was done, harvest was much too far away to continue on. Geek had an old Chevy truck and had hoped to get a job hauling grain. His hope didn't materialize. But at Geek's suggestion, we took off in his truck for Loveland, Colorado, to pick cherries. The cherries were there, but so were the skilled Hispanic laborers. One of them could pick more cherries in an hour than Geek or I could in a day. We couldn't make enough to buy our grub.

We gave up cherry picking and Geek went looking to buy a load of produce to take back to Kansas. In the meantime, I latched on to the mail carrier and rode up to Estes Park, Colorado, through the mountainous back roads. We came home by a more direct route through Big Thompson Canyon. This trip was my first to the mountains and a real adventure.

On our way back with a load of potatoes, Geek dropped me off at Lyle's farm near Kirk in Eastern Colorado.

After a few days there, I hitchhiked home. On that last jaunt I learned that farm hands in summer could not count on getting rides like a college student can during the school year. Nevertheless, I eventually made it.

# 60. Dug Wells

We moved and tried farming again for a while. But rocky fields were new to us as were dug wells.

The federal government tried during the mid-1930s to help destitute farmers with government loans obtained through the Farm and Home Administration. But with grain and livestock prices at rock bottom levels, not all farmers could make a go of it. The government foreclosed on many of the loans and then rented the farms to other destitute farmers.

Our landlord passed away in 1938, but his widow continued trying to run the farm. She was impossible to deal with, so we began looking elsewhere. Dad's health had deteriorated and his mind was failing by this time, so Oscar was running the farm. He had heard of government land that was available and located a farm in Eastern Kansas. We pulled up stakes and moved east in the spring of 1939. I was in college at the time, but I skipped classes a couple of days to help with the move. We hauled our stuff on our truck and trailers to our new home.

Land we had always farmed, was all dirt. You could drill a well a hundred feet deep or deeper and never hit a rock. But at some depth you hit a layer of sand that had water flowing through it, and there you stopped digging, sank a two-inch casing in the hole, set a sand point to filter the water, installed a pump, and you had an abundance of water.

Not so in on our new farm. The land was situated on top of bedrock with rocks cropping out over much of the area. Farmers laid out their fields in all shapes and sizes between rocky areas. That left lots of land to use as pasture or grow native prairie hay. Our wells—we had two—were dug into the bedrock, and we hauled water up in buckets on ropes. Looking down in the well, I saw debris floating on the water. I always felt that the water was contaminated.

We had a garden, but watering it from a dug well was not practical. The summer of 1939 produced a record drought in the area, so the garden as well as field crops were poor. We went deeper in the hole. I did not seek outside work that summer but stayed home, trying to help keep our heads above water.

Dad went to meet his Maker in the fall of that year. That left Mother, Mildred, and Oscar to hold down the home while I was away at school. I stayed home again the next summer to help.

But I never got used to plowing around rocks. And I didn't care for drawing water from a dug well.

# 61. Coming of Age

Kansas is supposed to be flat, but apparently no one told the surveyors for the Missouri Pacific Railroad when they laid out the section of their mainline from Ottawa to Lyndon. Coming west out of the Marais des Cygnes River Valley at Ottawa, a train has to climb the steepest grade on the line between St. Louis and the Rocky Mountains. The railroad crossed our field less than a half-mile south of our house, and this steep grade topped out at about the point where the track left our farm.

Every day around noon, a long freight train came up the grade huffing and puffing and blowing smoke and steam halfway to the sky. Gradually, it would lose speed until finally there were no more huffs. The train stalled.

The crew parted the train in the middle, pulled the front half onto a siding a mile or two west at the little town of Vassar, unhitched the locomotive and returned for the rear half. They pulled it into Vassar, coupled the train back together and headed for the Rockies.

The fact that the powerful steamer couldn't make the grade seemed incredible to me. My uncle Elmer pulled some of his line's best passenger trains, and he must have been good since railroads traditionally scheduled their best on the passenger runs. He adamantly stressed the superiority of steam over diesel locomotives, so I believed in him without question.

Early diesels used diesel electric power, which means that the engine drives a dynamo—which in turn drives the locomotive's electric motors. These had not proved entirely successful. However, later diesels with direct drives were doing well on passenger runs, so Uncle Elmer had to qualify his stand about diesels; they may make it on passenger runs but never on heavy freight trains.

One day about the time the Missouri Pacific freight was due to labor up the grade, we heard, instead of the usual huffing and puffing, a steady rumble. Coming up the track was a diesel locomotive of several sections with the daily freight train trailing behind it. By the time they reached the top of the grade, the diesel engines were groaning and not going fast enough to set any speed records, but they made it over the top and the train was on its way westward without stopping at Vassar.

We never again watched them part a train on the grade. The diesel had replaced the steam locomotive on the Missouri Pacific run. Could Uncle Elmer have been wrong?

By the time diesels had replaced steam engines on the Rock Island Railroad, my uncle had only a short time left before retirement and opted not to check out on diesels. He spent his last days of work jockeying cars in the Pratt switchyard with his beloved steam locomotives.

# 62. Times Change

I struggled through college. It wasn't easy. My freshman year was an experience to avoid. To save money, I did my own cooking, which wasn't so bad except that groceries—even for one—cost money, and I had none. By spring I was a nervous wreck. I couldn't muster the courage to return to college the following year.

Forrest was a mechanic for a motor freight line, and occasionally, although he didn't like to, he filled in as a driver. The old adage, "It's not what you know, it's who you know that counts," must be true. Forrest got me a job as a relief driver during the summer of 1937, and it certainly wasn't through my effort. But I welcomed the job. Rush season for the trucking industry in Kansas is in spring and summer, when farm work is at its peak. My job ran out in the fall, but I had saved enough money to tackle college again at mid-term the following January.

It was the following summer that I followed the harvest into Nebraska, and with the money I saved that summer I was still able to continue my education.

By the spring we had moved to Eastern Kansas, Dad's health was failing and so was his mental state. His care became quite a burden. Oscar had more than he could handle, so I stayed home the next two summers rather than follow the harvest as I had the summer before.

Staying home meant no cash for college. But by borrowing money, working at part-time jobs, and spending as little as possible, I hung on.

By the end of my junior year, Hitler was storming across Europe, and the United States was gearing up to counter the threat of a Nazi takeover. The industrial sector of the economy was booming. However, economic recovery on the farm was lagging.

I began my senior year of college in the fall of 1940. At that same time, the military draft began, and my number came up in the first drawing. I had planned on teaching high school math and science a few years before continuing my education, but the college asked that I take my Army physical in advance to determine if I qualified for military service. I did and passed with flying colors.

The teachers' placement program then removed my name from their rolls and returned my fee. The draft did not exempt teachers. However, it did defer college students in their senior year. Before the year was over, I was accepted for weather training at a civilian university as an Army Air Corps cadet non-pilot, and I did not have to answer the draft.

But by this time, Oscar had had enough of fruitless endeavors at farming. He enrolled in a vocational school to learn sheet metal work and tool and die making. He landed a job with Cessna Aircraft, sold off the farm equipment, and moved with Mother and Mildred to Wichita.

Shortly after the family moved and I entered graduate school as a cadet, the Japanese bombed Pearl Harbor. Then the economy really surged. Lyle began making a real profit at farming, and Forrest was employed by Remington Arms in Denver. Mildred was working for a pharmaceutical firm in Wichita. We were all involved in the country's defense effort. For the Snyders and most of the rest of the country, the Depression was over.

I finished my cadet training, received my commission as a 2nd Lieutenant, and moved to Will Rogers Air Base in Oklahoma City. I married the girl of my dreams, and we rented an apartment. The pantry was as bare as Mother Hubbard's cupboard. At the Humpty Dumpty grocery down the street, we latched onto a new gadget that had just entered the scene. It was a wire basket on wheels, and you shoved it around the store to haul your groceries. We needed about everything: matches, toothpicks, spices, salt, pepper, baking powder, soda, sugar, flour, shortening, soap, starch, bleach, cleanser, toilet paper, coffee, wax paper, and you name it.

*Our first grocery list*

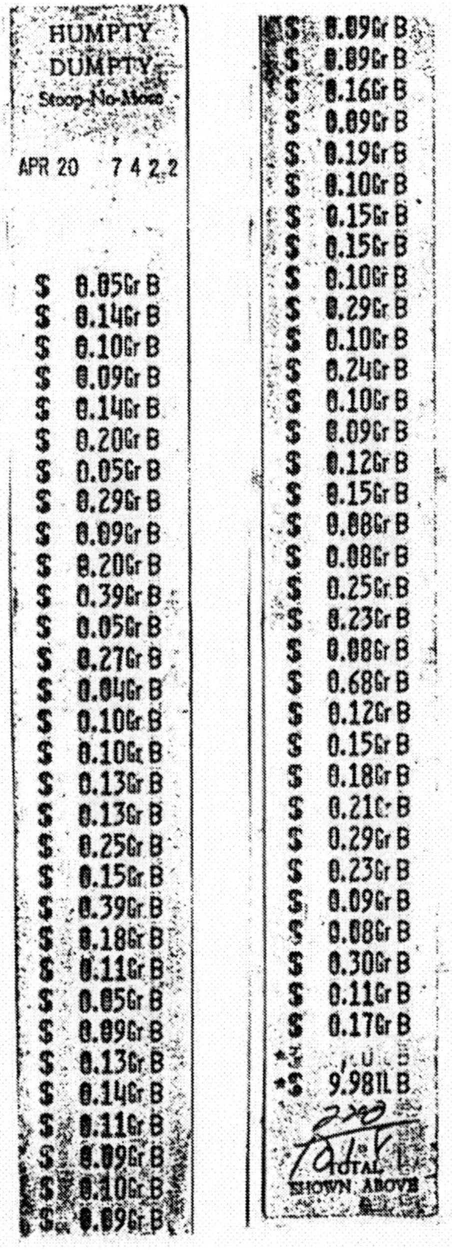
HUMPTY
DUMPTY
Stoop-No-More

APR 20 7 4 2 2

$ 0.05Gr B
$ 0.14Gr B
$ 0.10Gr B
$ 0.09Gr B
$ 0.14Gr B
$ 0.20Gr B
$ 0.05Gr B
$ 0.29Gr B
$ 0.09Gr B
$ 0.20Gr B
$ 0.39Gr B
$ 0.05Gr B
$ 0.27Gr B
$ 0.04Gr B
$ 0.10Gr B
$ 0.10Gr B
$ 0.13Gr B
$ 0.13Gr B
$ 0.25Gr B
$ 0.15Gr B
$ 0.39Gr B
$ 0.18Gr B
$ 0.11Gr B
$ 0.05Gr B
$ 0.09Gr B
$ 0.13Gr B
$ 0.14Gr B
$ 0.11Gr B
$ 0.09Gr B
$ 0.10Gr B
$ 0.09Gr B
$ 0.09Gr B
$ 0.09Gr B
$ 0.16Gr B
$ 0.09Gr B
$ 0.19Gr B
$ 0.10Gr B
$ 0.15Gr B
$ 0.15Gr B
$ 0.10Gr B
$ 0.29Gr B
$ 0.10Gr B
$ 0.24Gr B
$ 0.10Gr B
$ 0.09Gr B
$ 0.12Gr B
$ 0.15Gr B
$ 0.08Gr B
$ 0.08Gr B
$ 0.25Gr B
$ 0.23Gr B
$ 0.08Gr B
$ 0.68Gr B
$ 0.12Gr B
$ 0.15Gr B
$ 0.18Gr B
$ 0.21Gr B
$ 0.29Gr B
$ 0.23Gr B
$ 0.09Gr B
$ 0.08Gr B
$ 0.30Gr B
$ 0.11Gr B
$ 0.17Gr B
*$ [illegible]
*$ 9.98TL B
TOTAL
SHOWN ABOVE

Our first cash register receipt

And of course, we bought some food.

When we rolled the shopping cart up to the cash register, the cashier's eyes got as big as saucers. The grocery bill added up to $9.98, plus 20 cents tax, a $10.18 total.

I doubt that the cashier even had a gun, so I wasn't too concerned about his comment, "If my wife did that to me, I'd shoot her."

## The End

978-0-595-35130-5
0-595-35130-1

Printed in the United States
35599LVS00003B/161